COLOR SAINT PAUL

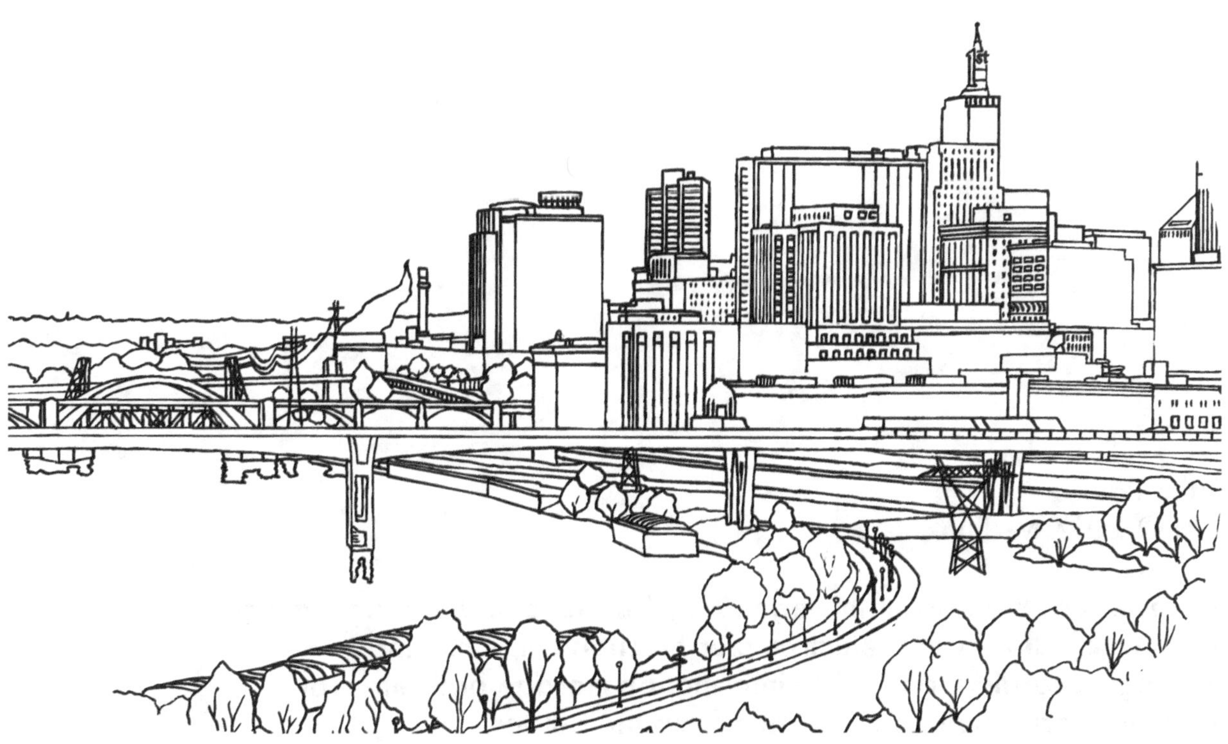

M. Funk

Color Saint Paul
Copyright © 2017 M. Funk

ISBN-10: 0-9983016-1-2
ISBN-13: 978-0-9983016-1-7

Published by Local Color Books
www.LocalColorBooks.com

Printed in the USA

If you plan to decorate the following pages
with marker, please feel free to
tear this page out and place it beneath
your work to prevent color from bleeding
through to the next page.

Enjoy!

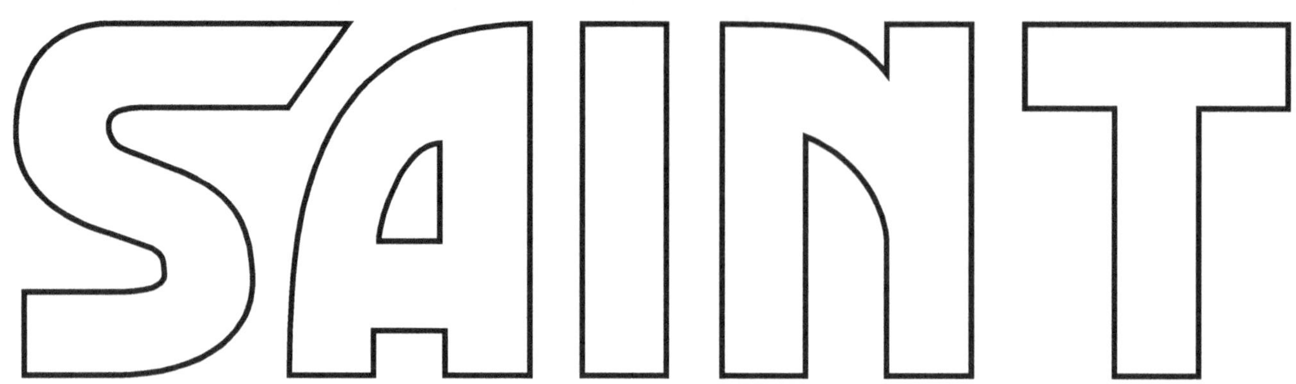

SAINT
Landmark Center 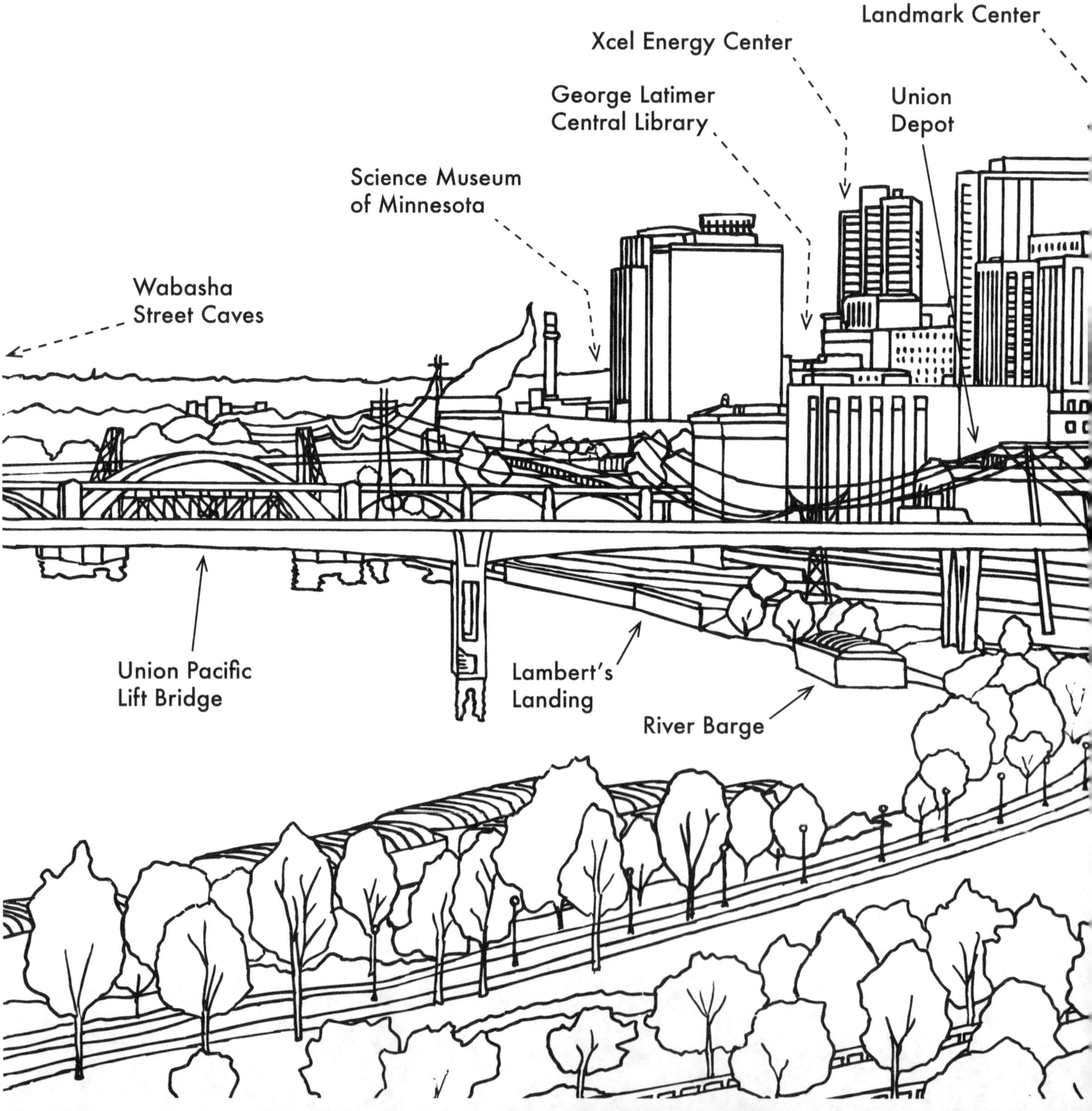
Xcel Energy Center
George Latimer
Central Library
Union
Depot
Science Museum
of Minnesota
Wabasha
Street Caves
Union Pacific
Lift Bridge
Lambert's
Landing
River Barge

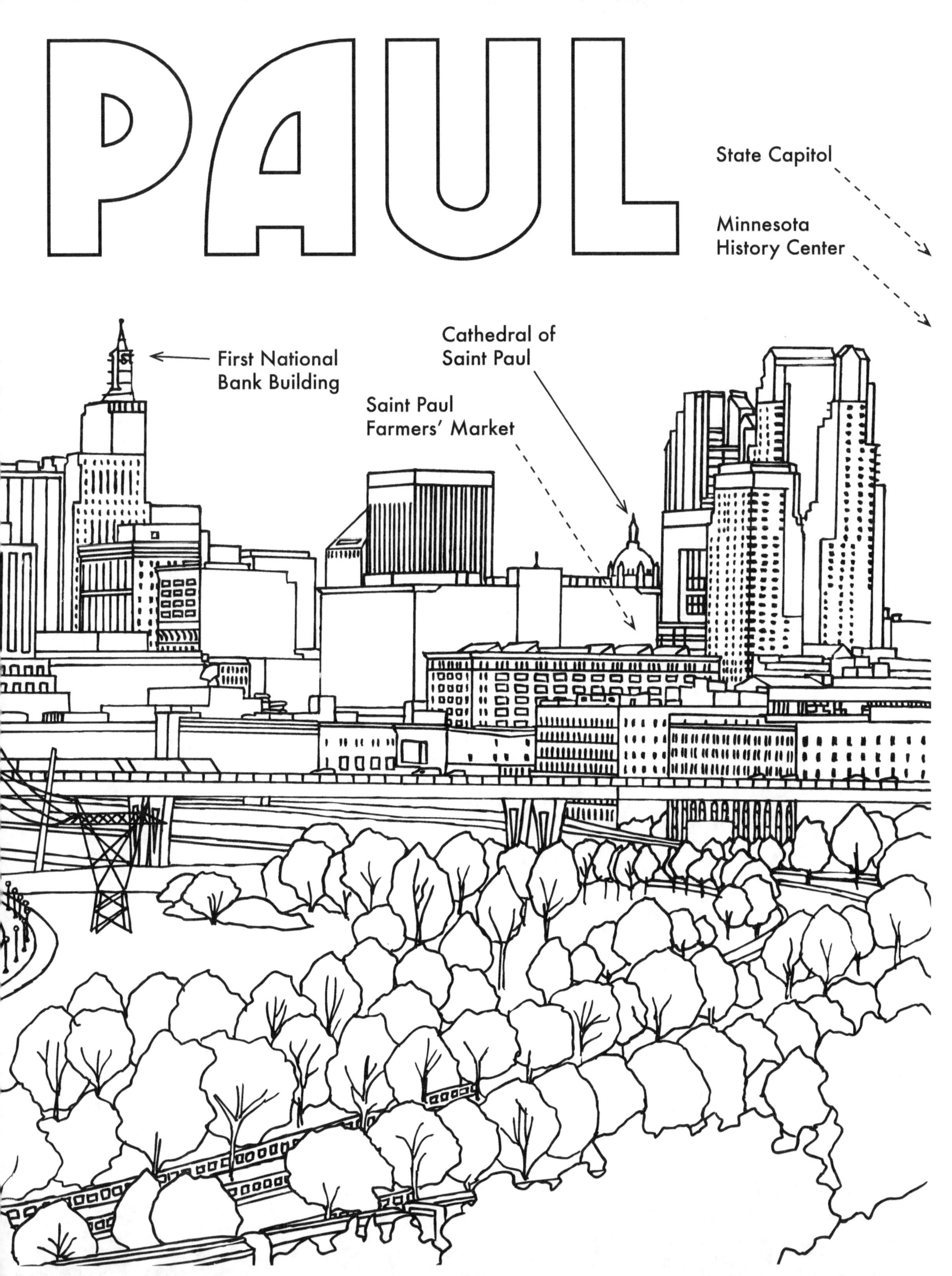

PAUL
State Capitol
Minnesota History Center
First National Bank Building
Cathedral of Saint Paul
Saint Paul Farmers' Market

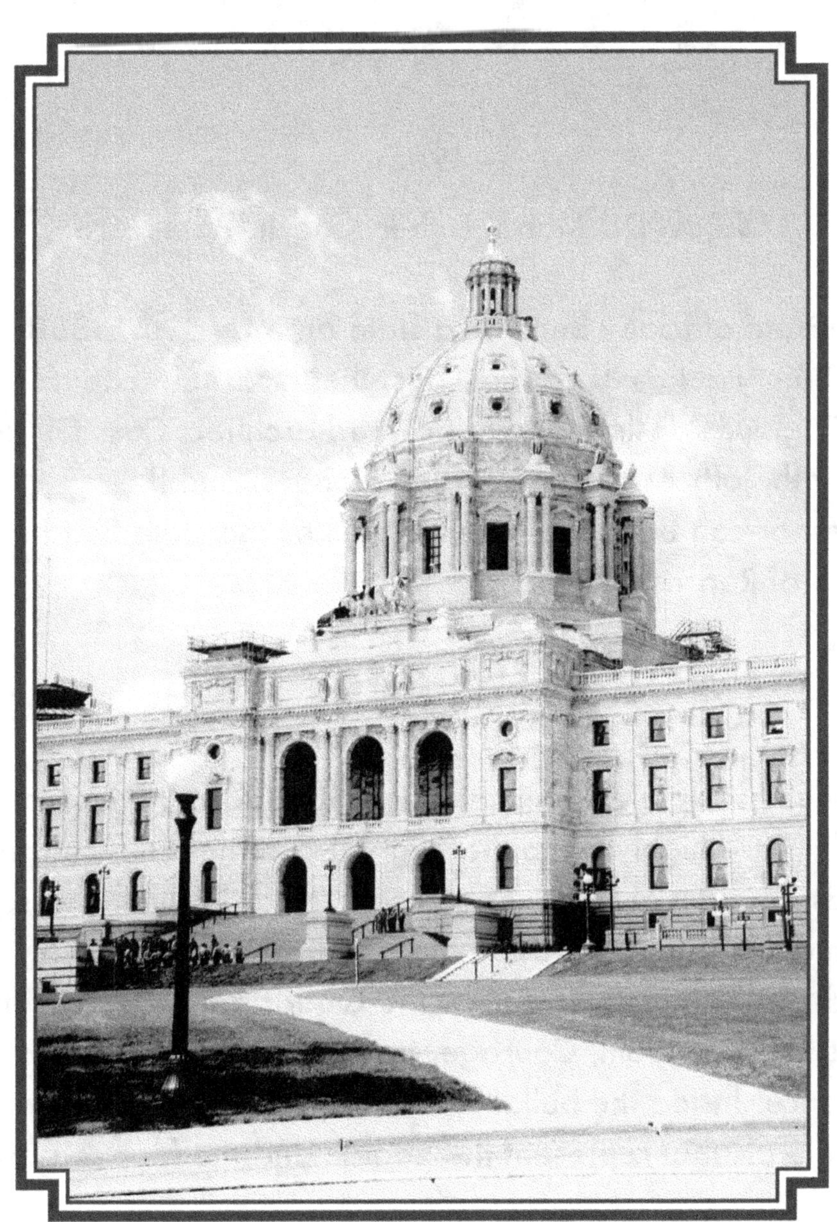

MINNESOTA STATE CAPITOL

- 1905 -

75 Rev. Dr. Martin Luther King Jr. Boulevard

Minnesota officially became a state on May 11th, 1858, with Saint Paul as its capitol. This, the third state capitol building, was designed by renowned architect Cass Gilbert. Today the offices of the Attorney General and the Governor can be found here, as well as the state Senate and House of Representatives.

- FUN FACT -

The many sculptures and paintings that adorn the capitol building are highly symbolic. High above the main entrance stands a gold-leaf statue of a chariot pulled by four horses (a Quadriga) that represent the forces of nature: Earth, Wind, Fire, and Water. Below the Quadriga pose six statues that signify Wisdom, Courage, Bounty, Truth, Integrity, and Prudence. Inside the building, the ceilings are decorated with murals that represent the zodiac and the four seasons.

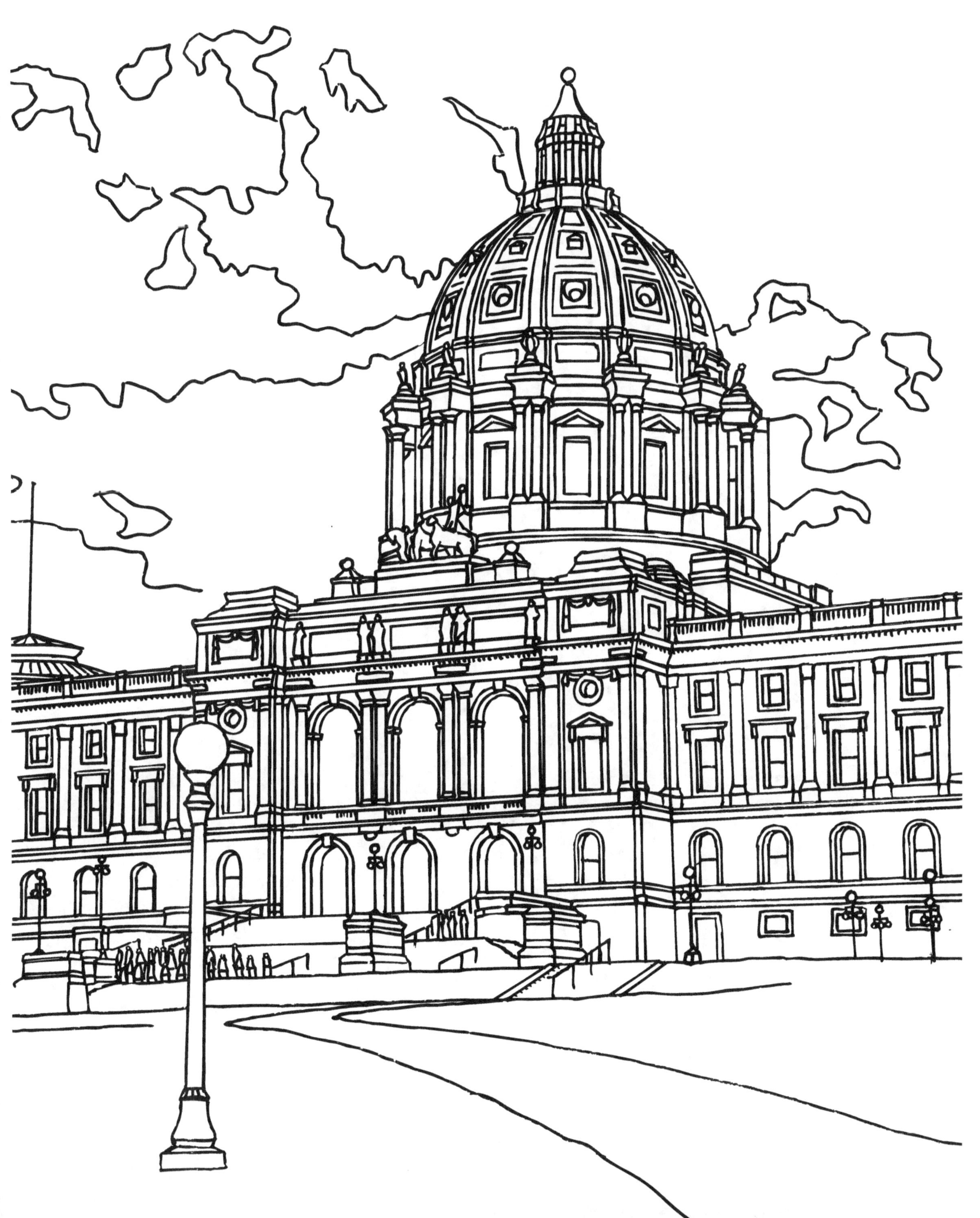

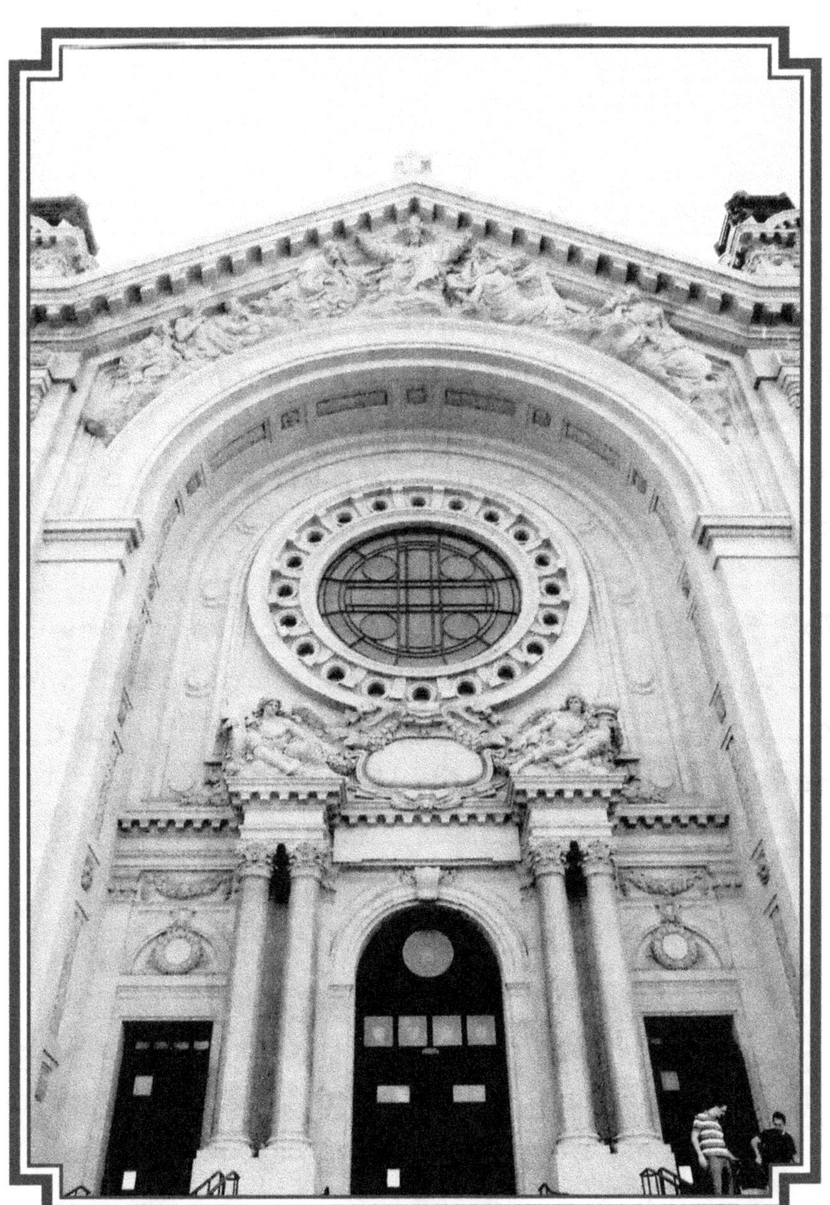

CATHEDRAL OF SAINT PAUL

- 1915 -

239 Selby Avenue

The Cathedral of Saint Paul was designed in the Beaux-Arts style by French Architect Emmanuel Louis Masqueray. Many gifted artisans and craftsmen contributed to the richly decorated interior carvings, statues, paintings, and ornamentation.

In 1958, Archbishop William O. Brady performed the Rite of Consecration at the Cathedral. Its consecration led to formal recognition of the church as an "edifice of merit," and a premier place of worship in the US.

- FUN FACT -

It was Father Lucien Galtier who established a chapel here in 1841 and placed the community (then known as Pig's Eye) under the patronage of Saint Paul. Eventually the name caught on, and Pig's Eye became the city of Saint Paul.

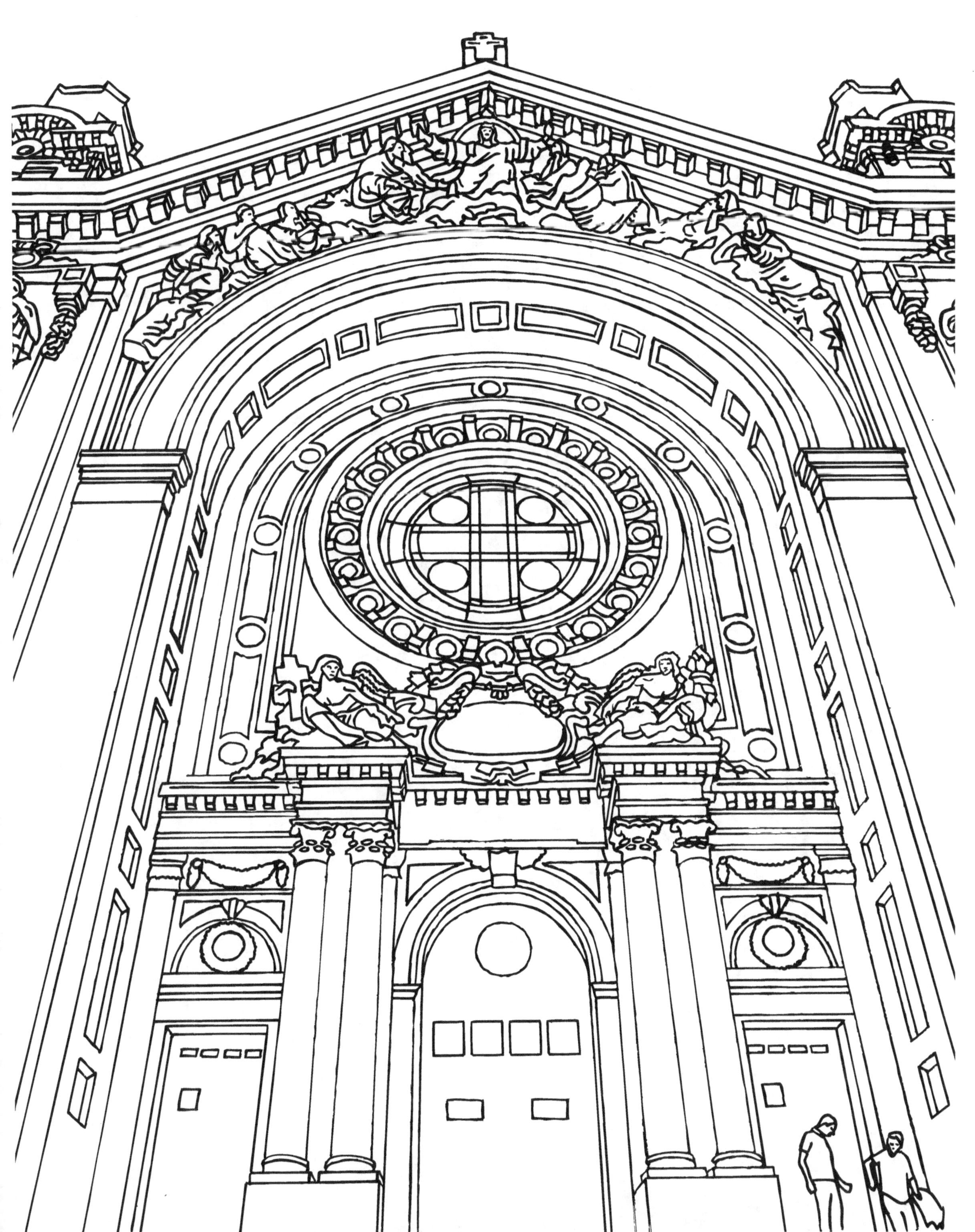

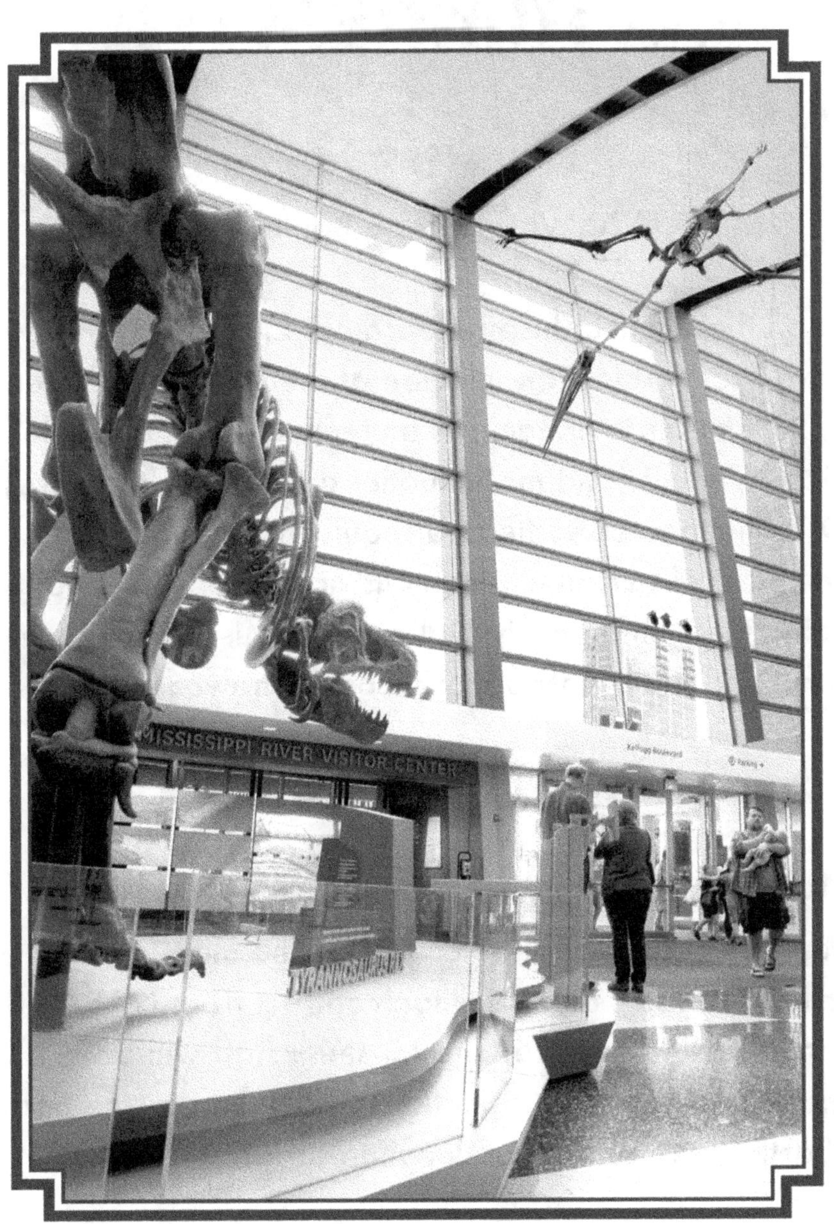

MISSISSIPPI RIVER VISITOR CENTER
TYRANNOSAURUS
Kellogg Boulevard
Parking

SCIENCE MUSEUM OF MINNESOTA

- 1999 -

120 West Kellogg Boulevard

"Turn on the science: Inspire learning. Inform policy. Improve lives." This is the mission of the Minnesota Science Museum. The museum focuses on technology, natural history, physical sciences, and mathematics education. It features an IMAX/Omnitheater dome and regularly hosts traveling shows. Several permanent exhibits are always on display, including the Human Body Gallery, the Mississippi River Gallery, and the Dinosaurs and Fossils showcase.

- FUN FACT -

Thanks to their excellent reputation for making science concepts inspirational and accessible, the museum was awarded a 5-year, $14.5 million contract from NASA's research division in 2016. The Museum staff will be partnering with several institutions to develop a free Space and Earth Informal STEM Education program.

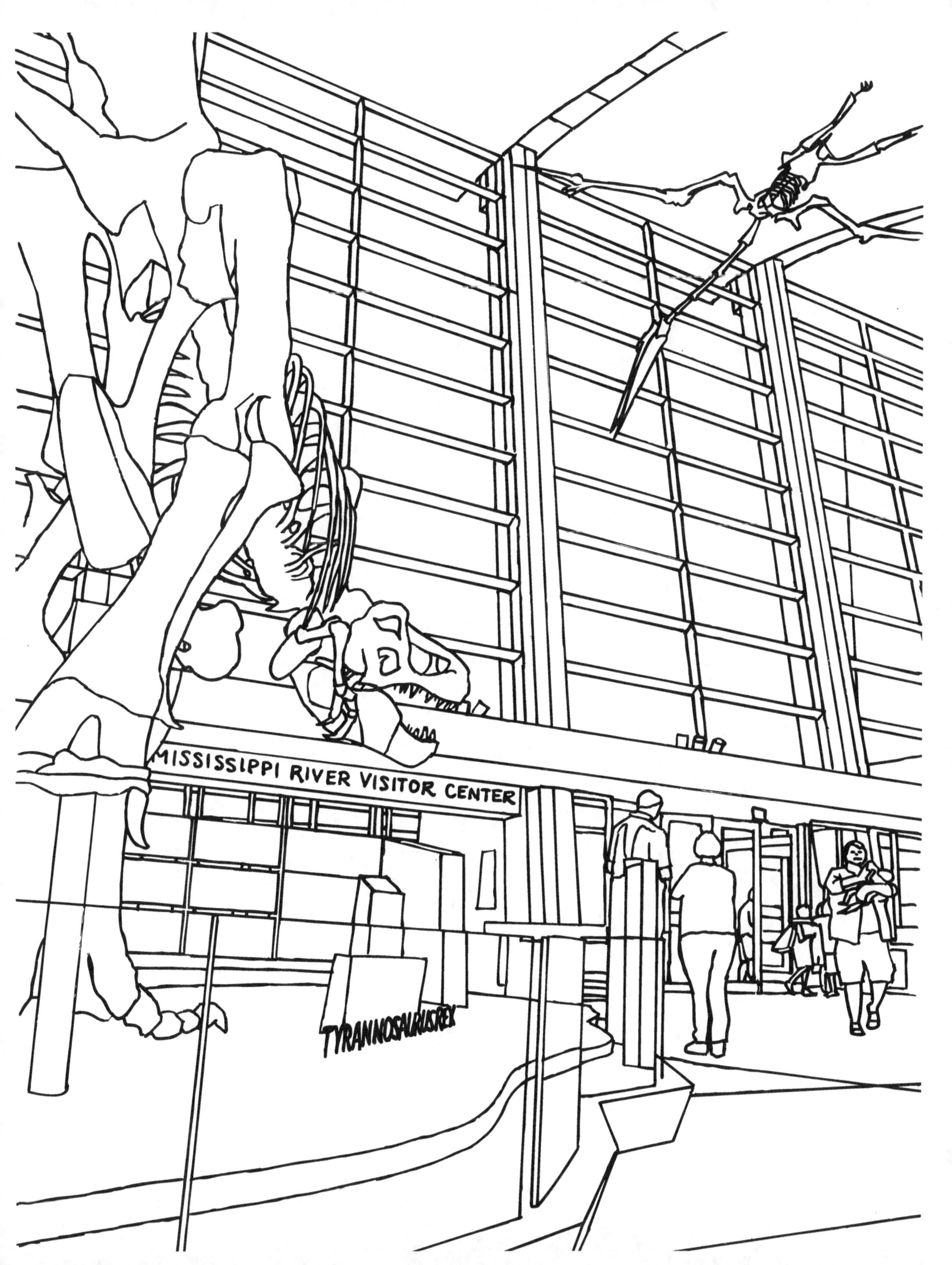

MISSISSIPPI RIVER VISITOR CENTER
TYRANNOSAURUS REX

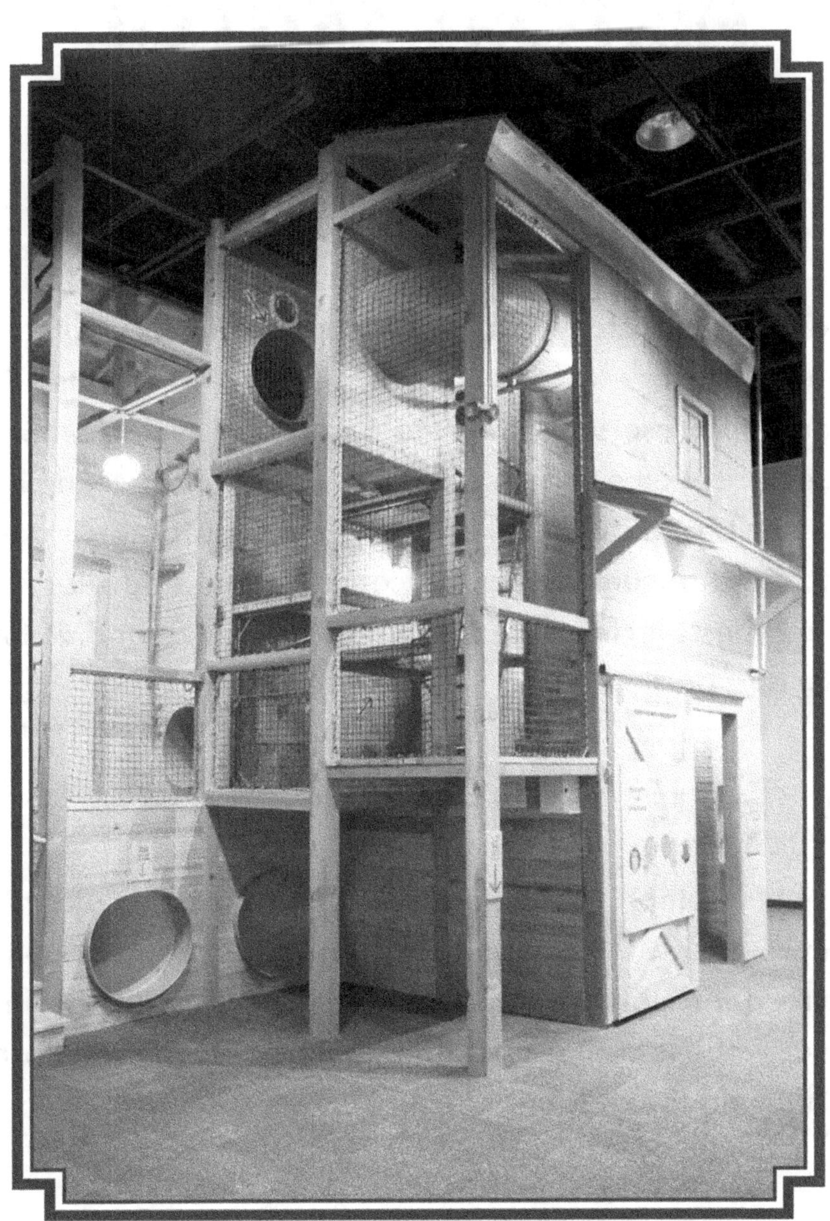

MINNESOTA HISTORY CENTER

- 1992 -

345 West Kellogg Boulevard

The Minnesota History Center is the headquarters of the Minnesota Historical Society (established in 1849). Its mission is to preserve Minnesota's stories in every form. The Center is home to several year-round and traveling public exhibits, an extensive library, underground storage of artifacts and documents, and a conservation laboratory. It regularly hosts lectures, performances, political and cultural events, and parties.

- FUN FACT -

One of the author's favorite exhibits at the Minnesota History Center is Grainland! Children (and scrappy adults) may crawl through the steps and slides of a replica grain elevator while learning about the journey of soy and corn from the field to the table.

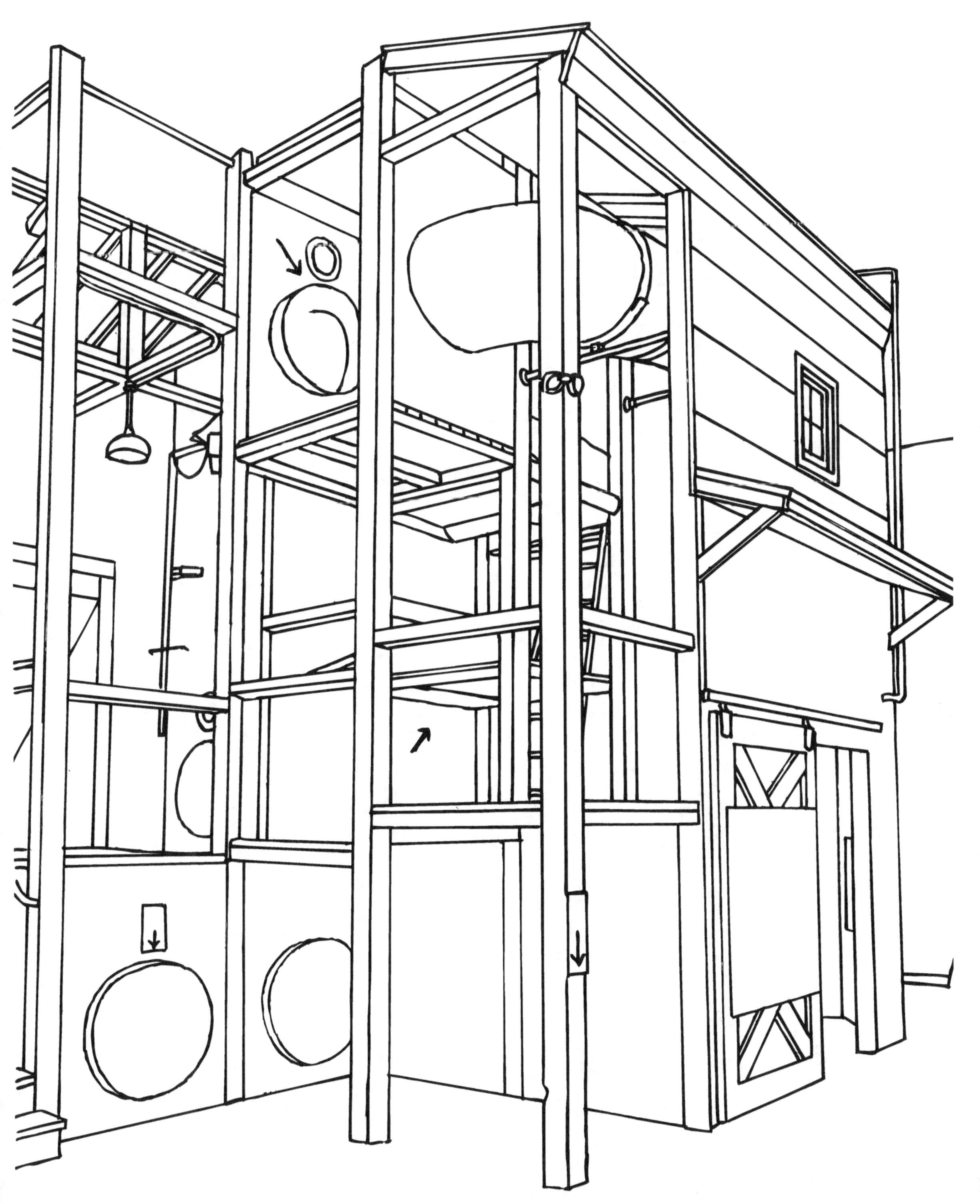

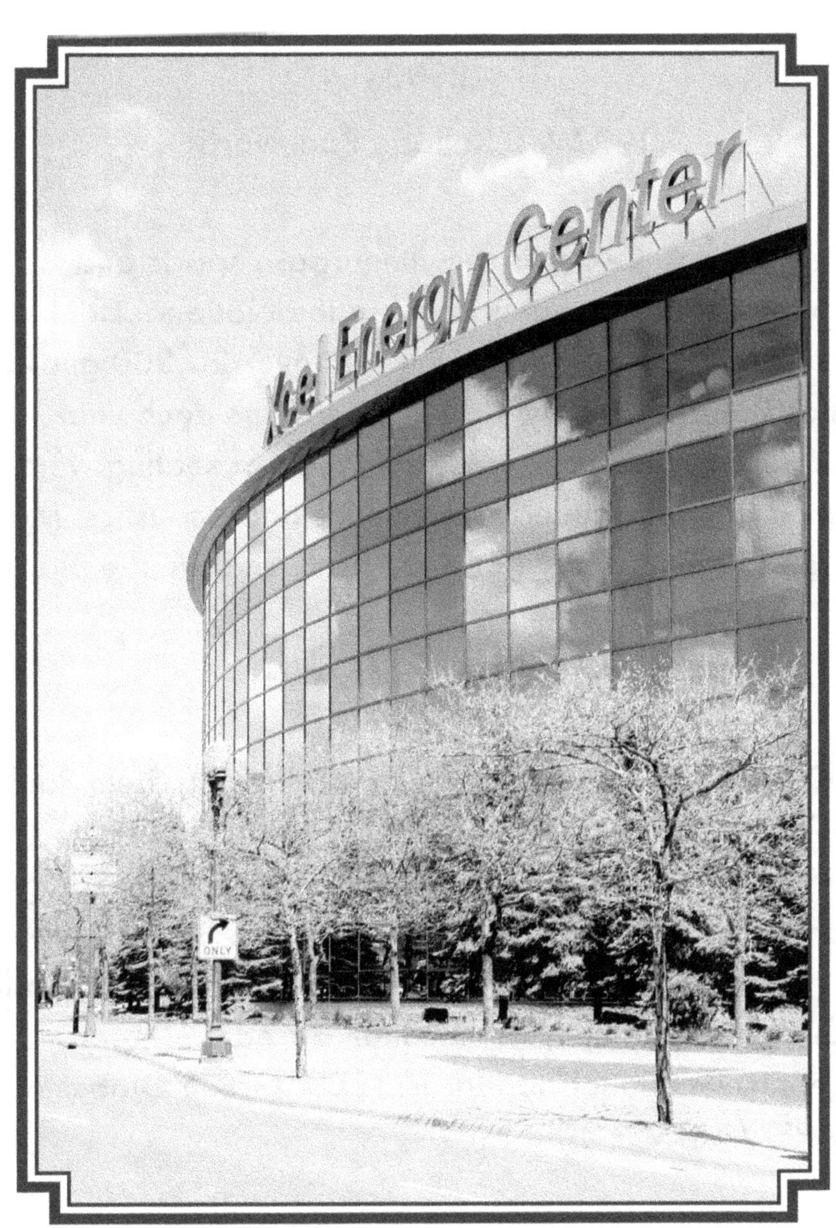
Xcel Energy Center

XCEL ENERGY CENTER

- 2000 -

199 West Kellogg Boulevard

The Xcel Energy Center is a multi-purpose sports and entertainment arena that is home to the National Hockey League's Minnesota Wild. It can seat over 20,000 guests, and hosts approximately 1.5 million visitors each year. Its wide-open concourses and four levels of seating were designed to create superior sight lines and acoustics. Many visitors confirm that there are no "bad" seats in the place.

- FUN FACT -

In 2009 the Xcel Energy Center and adjoining Saint Paul RiverCenter set a goal to become regional leaders in sustainability. Over the course of five years, the building and its operations underwent rigorous changes. By 2014, the Xcel Energy Center was the first such complex in the world to achieve sustainability certification based on three different international standards: LEED, Green Globes, and APEX/ASTM.

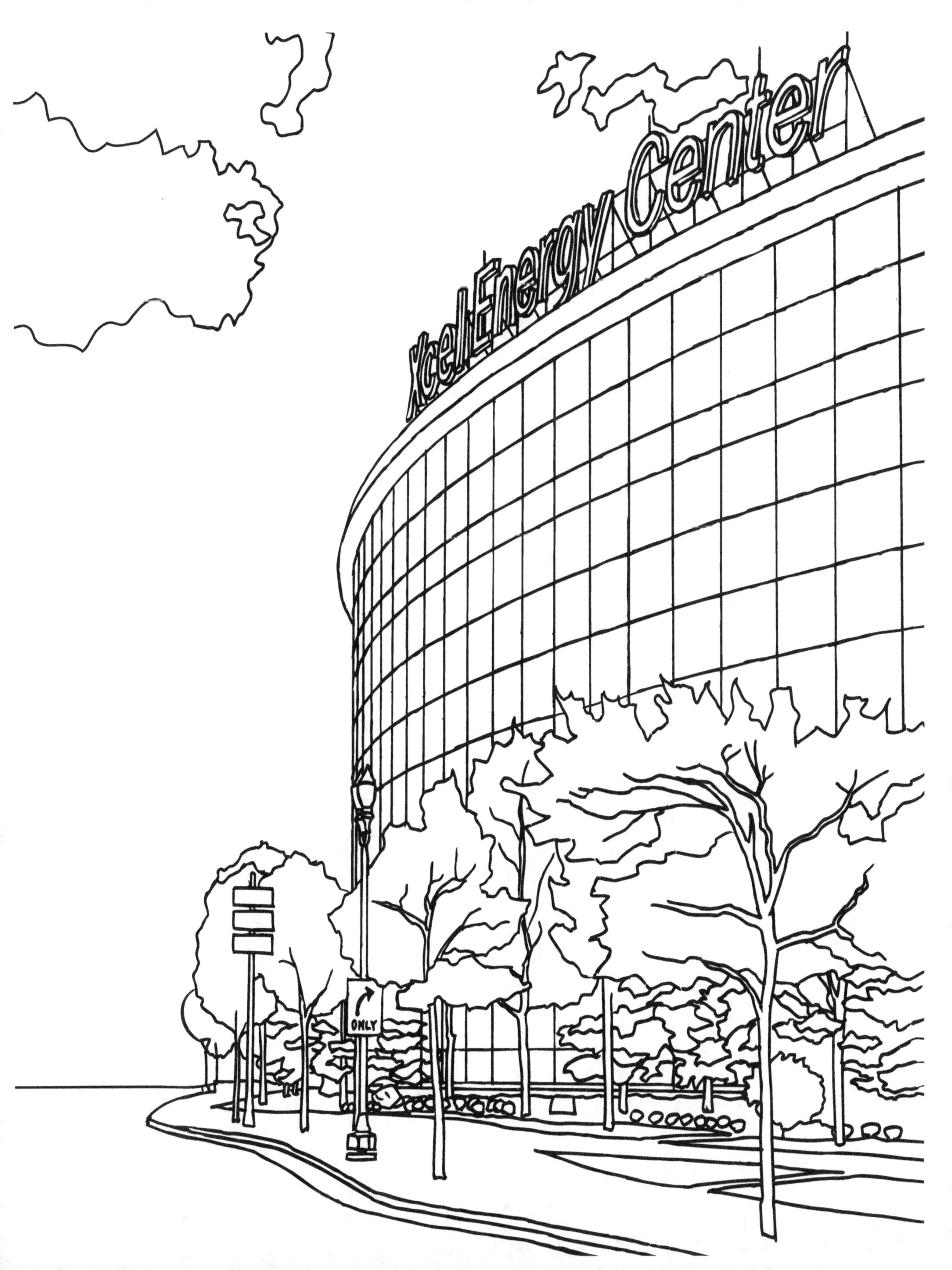

Xcel Energy Center
ONLY

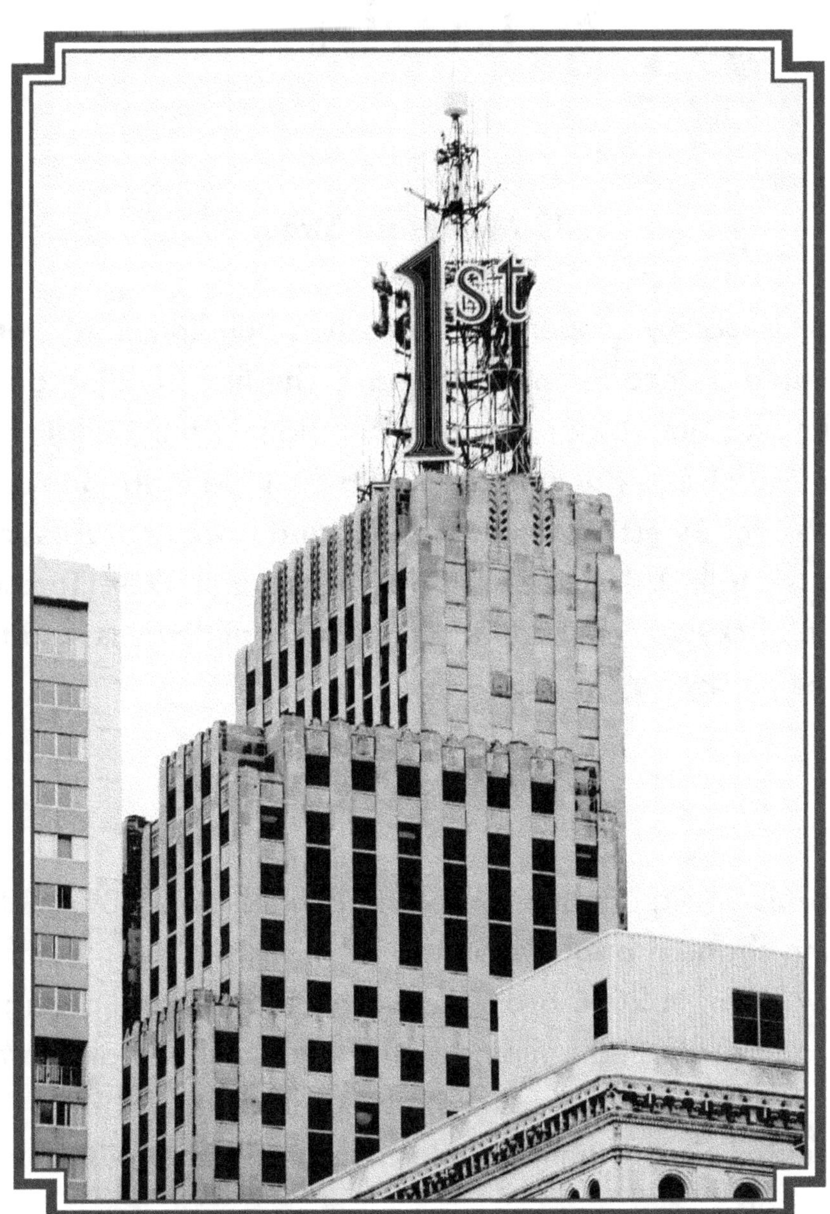

FIRST NATIONAL BANK BUILDING

- 1931 -

332 Minnesota Street

This art deco skyscraper is actually two buildings that were completed a decade and half apart. The first building on this site was the 16-story "east" Merchants Bank Building. When Merchants Bank merged with First National Bank, the 32-story "west" tower was built, and it was notable for being the tallest skyscraper in Saint Paul until 1987. The small section of skyway that connects the two buildings is said to be the first skyway in Saint Paul.

- FUN FACT -

The iconic 1st sign on the top of the First National Bank Building shone a bright neon red for nearly 80 years before a snow storm in 2016 broke a quarter of its neon lighting tubes and prompted building authorities to shut it off. Later that year, the sign was relit with LED bulbs and a bonus feature: the sign's lighting pattern could be controlled by a phone app.

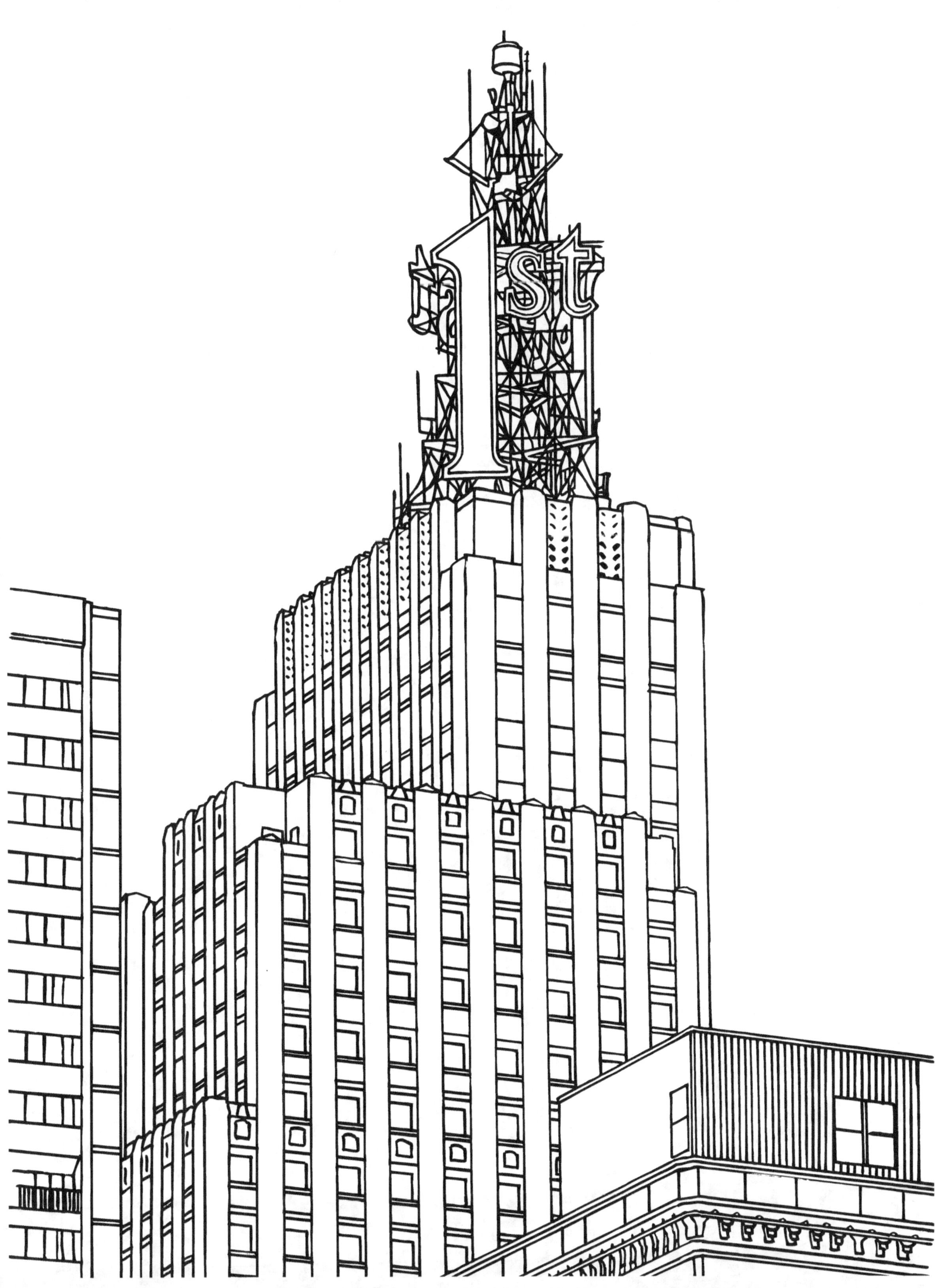

1st

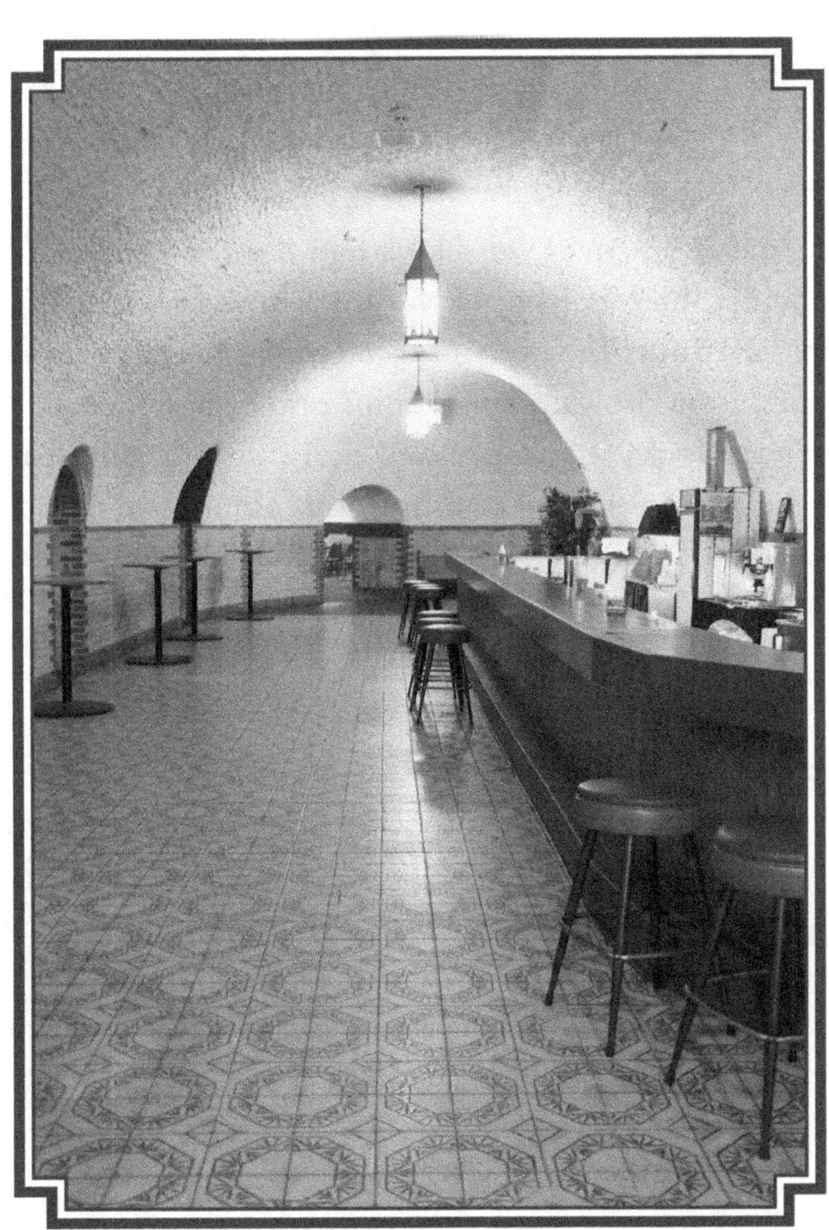

WABASHA STREET CAVES

- 1840s -

215 South Wabasha Street

These man-made caves were built into the sandstone bluffs across the Mississippi River from downtown Saint Paul in the 1840s. They have served many purposes over the years, from growing mushrooms and aging cheese to accommodating a speakeasy and a disco. Today the caves are home to a restaurant and bar that feature live music and lively swing dancing.

- FUN FACT -

During the 1920s and '30s the Caves were a popular gangster hangout. Here, shady characters could go about their illicit business and late-night poker games (some of which were rumored to have turned deadly). Present-day visitors to the Caves have reported run-ins with ghostly apparitions; one in particular wears a classic pinstripe suit, a Panama hat, and wing tip shoes.

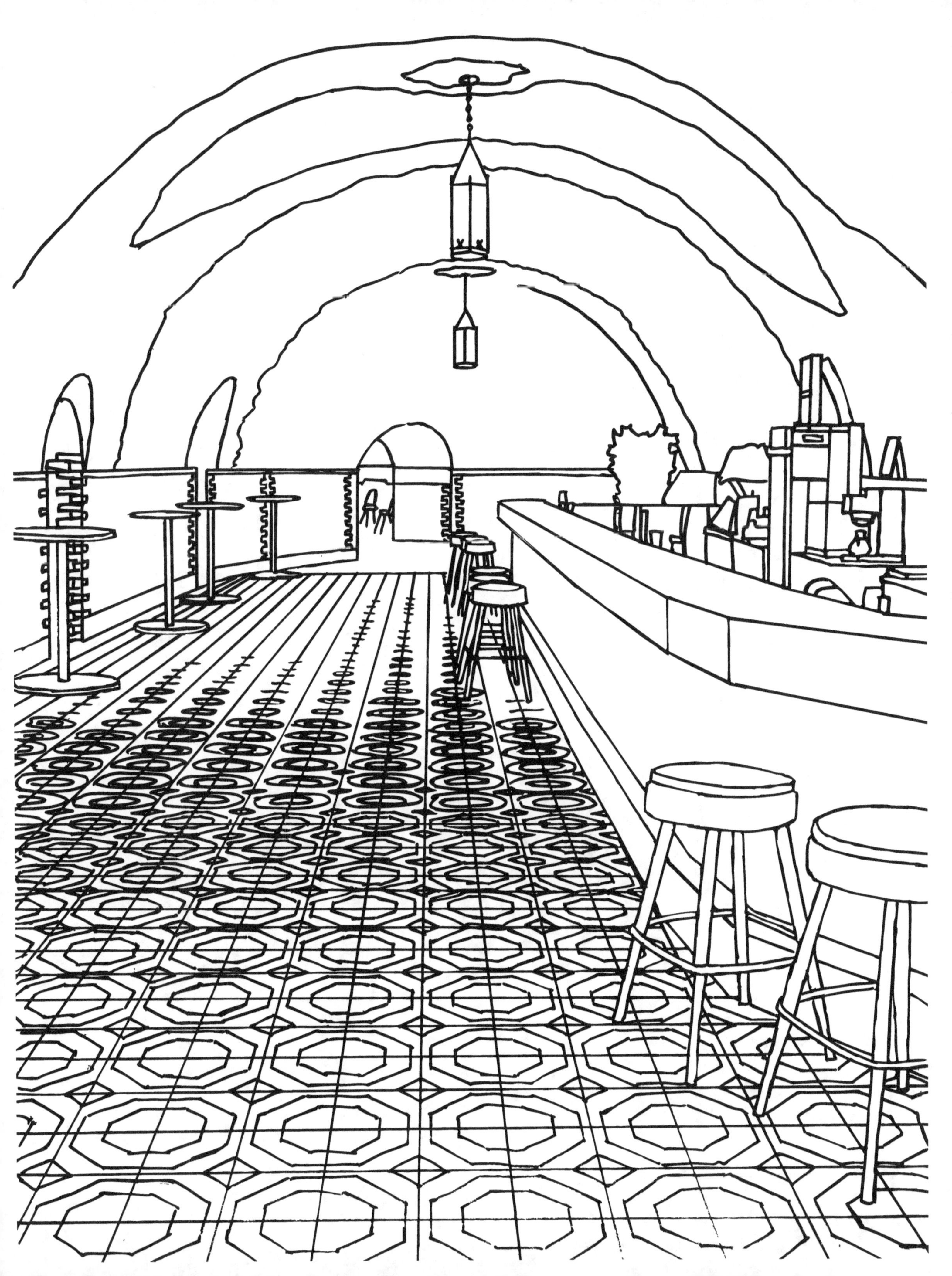

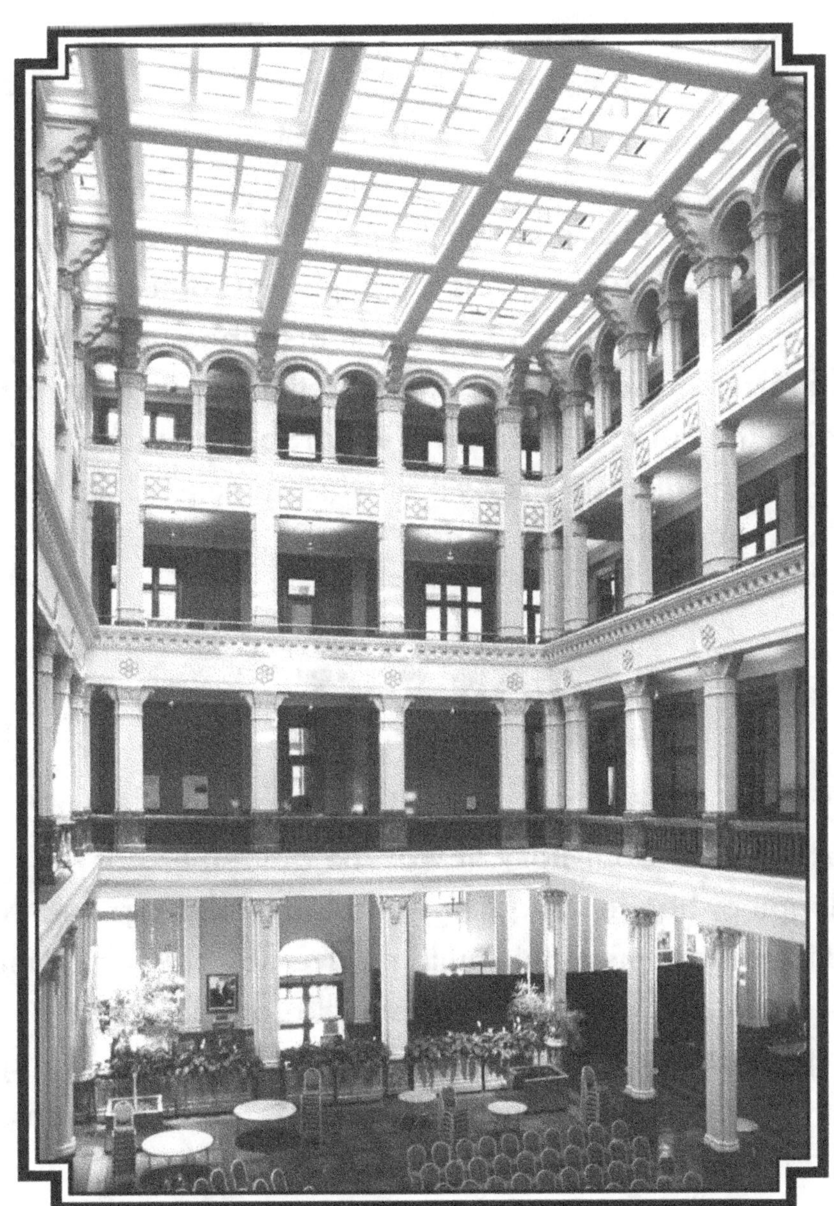

LANDMARK CENTER

- 1902 -

75 West 5th Street

Landmark Center, also known as the Old Federal Courts building, originally served as the city's post office, custom house, and court house. Over the years it became the headquarters for all federal offices in the Upper Midwest, including the FBI and the New Deal programs of the 1930s. Today the building serves as a downtown cultural center, housing a number of arts and non-profit agencies, and hosting private events.

– FUN FACT –

The Prohibition Era (1920–1933) was one of the most lawless times in US history. It was the golden era of bootlegging, booze-smuggling, and bank-robbing, and the upstairs courtrooms of this building overflowed with criminal cases. Ironically, famous gangsters like John Dillinger, George "Babyface" Nelson, and the Barker-Karpis Gang rarely saw the inside of these courtrooms. This was thanks to crooked deals with the local authorities.

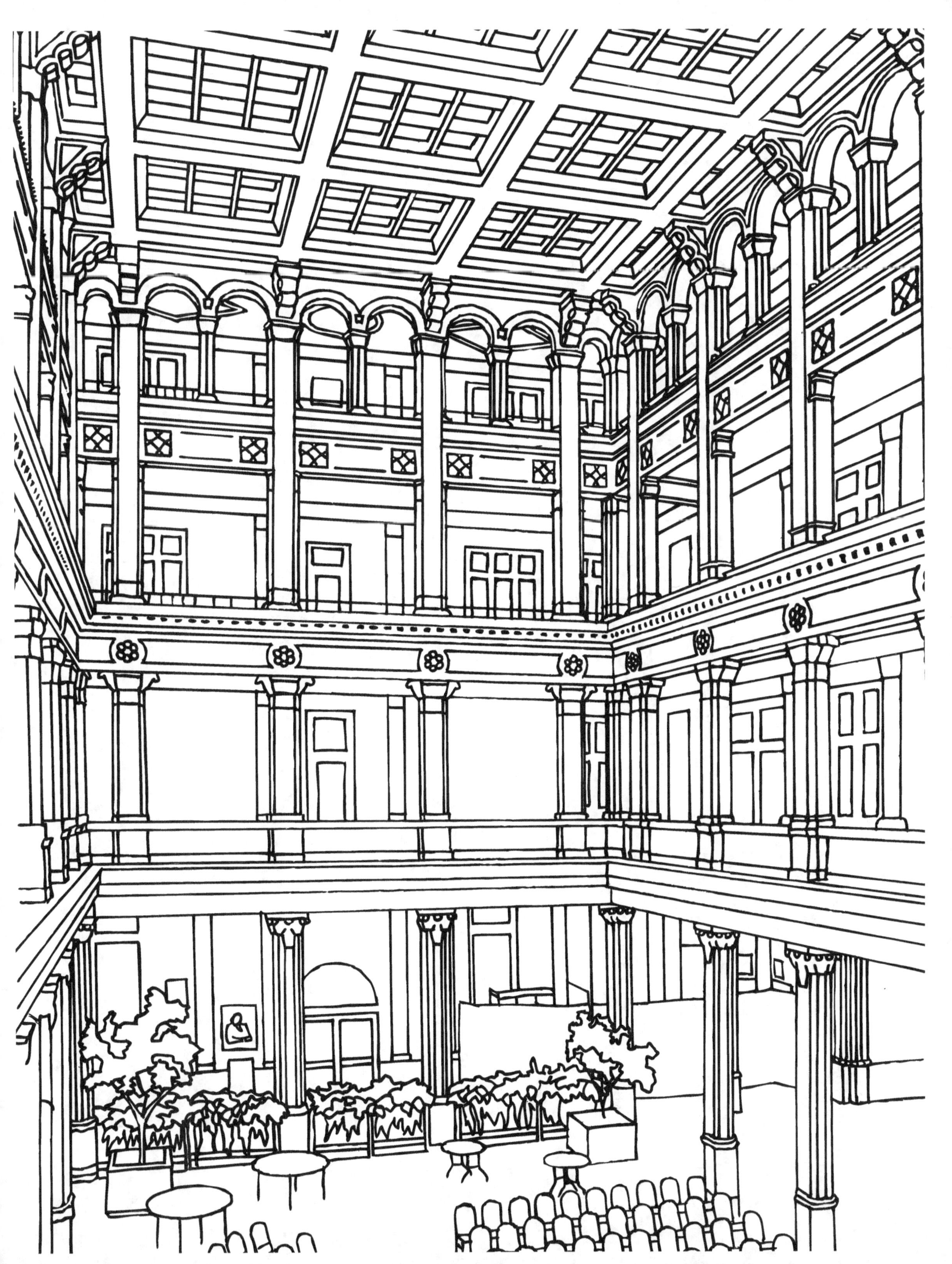

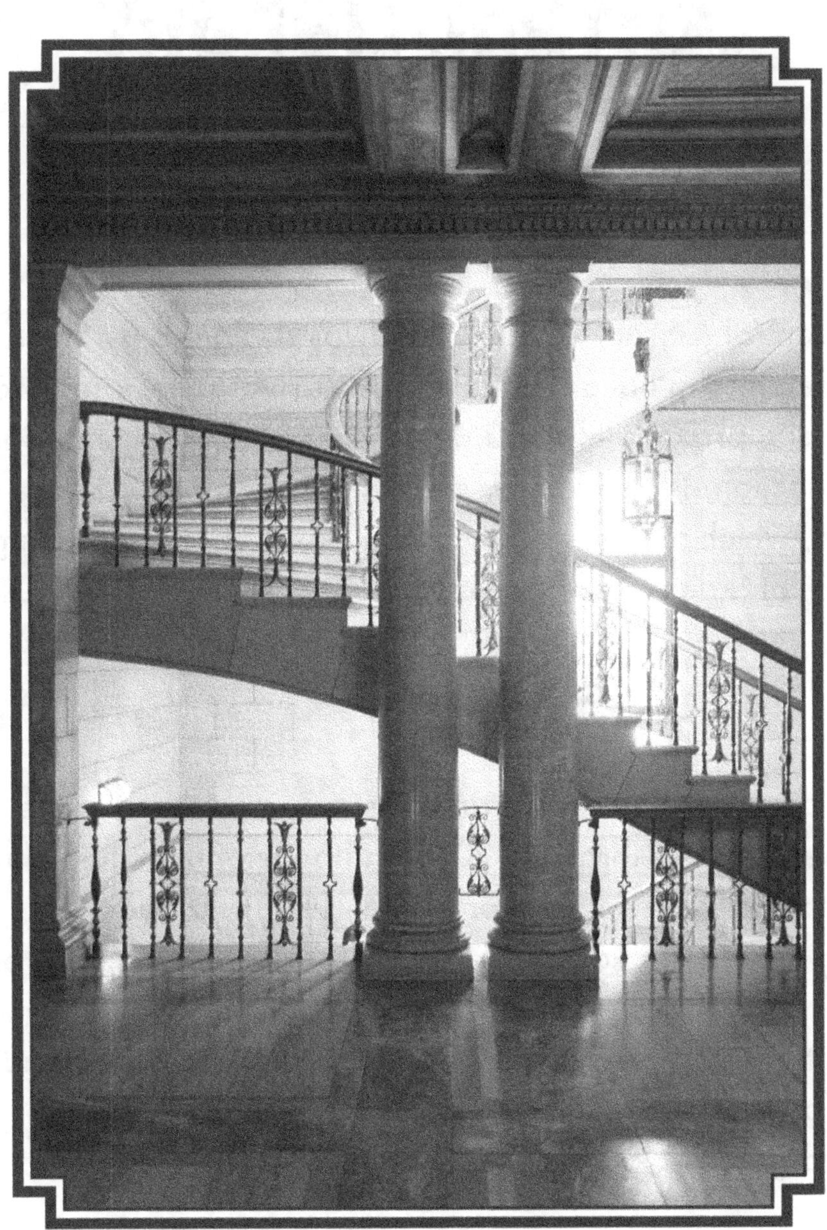

GEORGE LATIMER CENTRAL LIBRARY

- 1917 -

90 West 4th Street

The Central Library of Saint Paul was designed by Electus Litchfield in the Italian Renaissance Revival style. The library houses approximately 350,000 books and other materials in its collection. It also houses the city's first "maker" space for adults, which features a 3D printer, laser cutter, recording studio, and design software stations.

- FUN FACT -

The Saint Paul Central Library was renamed the George Latimer Central Library in 2014, in honor of the city's longest consecutively-serving mayor (1976–1990). In addition to being the mayor, Latimer spent 14 years on the Friends of the Library Board and helped raise funds to support library collections and programs. One of his goals as a city leader was for every child in Minnesota to be able to read by 3rd grade.

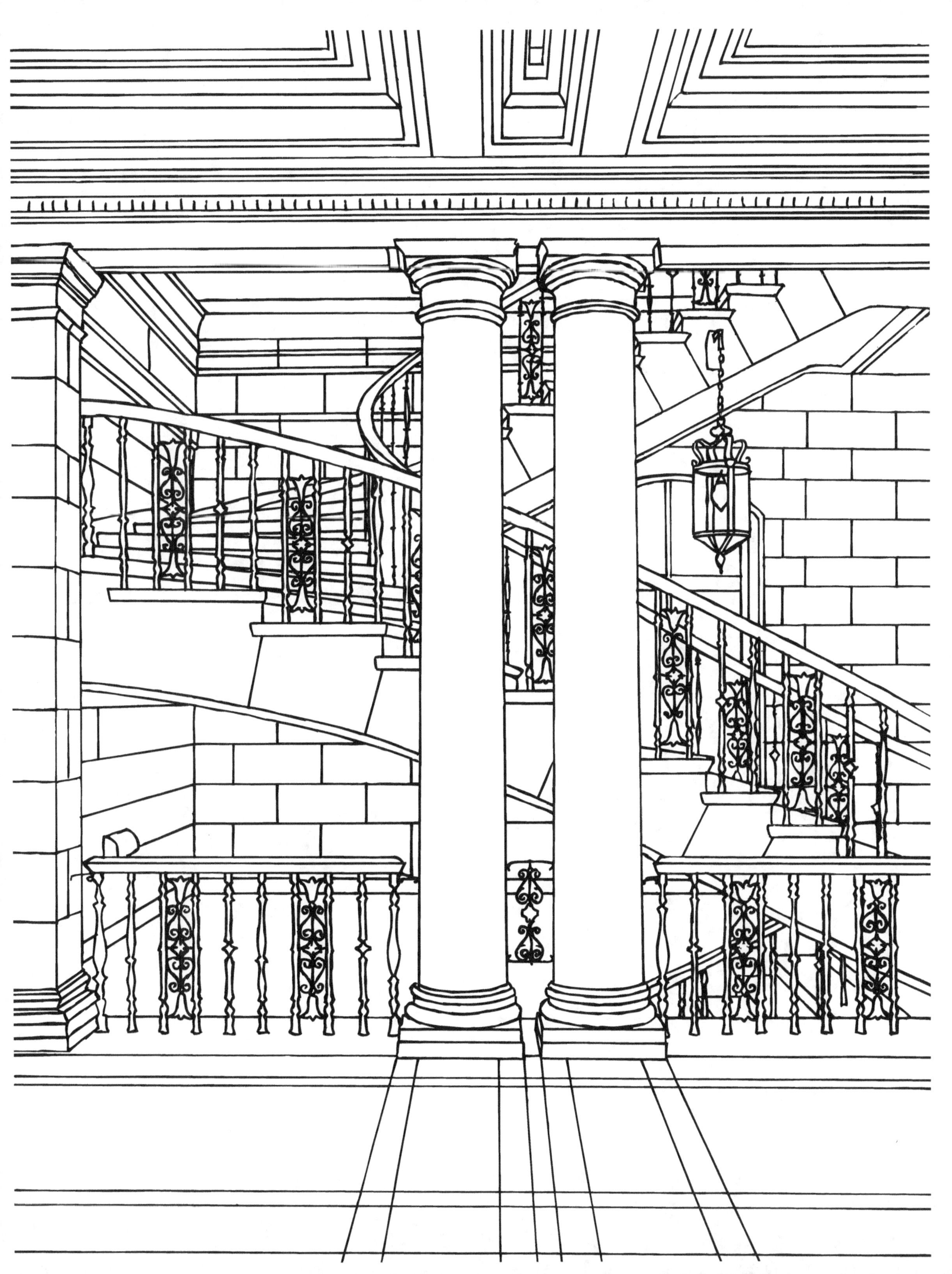

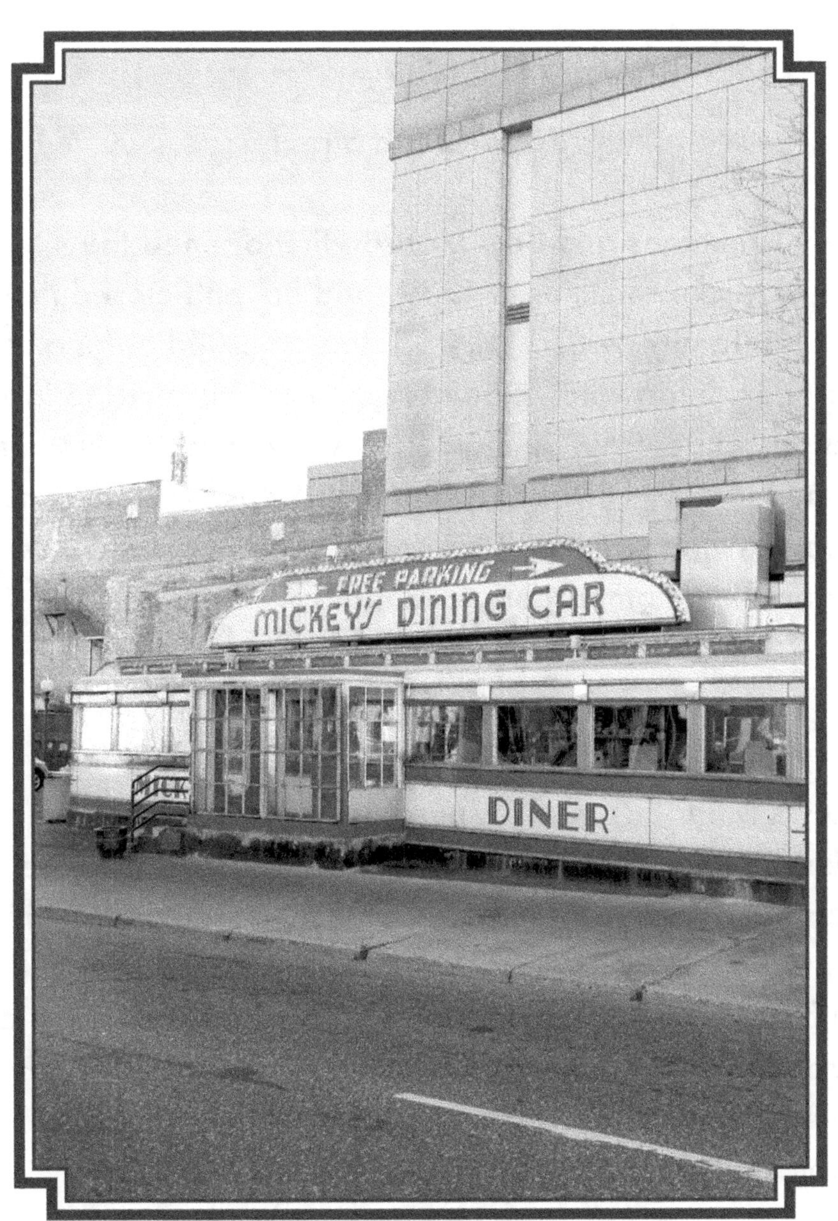

FREE PARKING
MICKEY'S DINING CAR
DINER

MICKEY'S DINER

- 1939 -

36 West 9th Street

Mickey Crimmons and Bert Mattson first opened the doors of Mickey's Diner in 1939, and haven't closed them since. This family-owned 24/365 diner, nestled among the skyscrapers in downtown Saint Paul, was designed to look like a passenger-train dining car. It was one of the first diners designed in the Art Deco style in the 1930s. Visitors can still stop by at any time of the day or night for pancakes, mulligan stew, hamburgers, and malts.

- FUN FACT -

Mickey's Diner has made a number of appearances in movies, TV shows, and the news. Most notably, the diner appeared in scenes from the *Mighty Ducks* movie franchise, *Jingle All the Way*, and *A Prairie Home Companion*. It has been featured on travel and food television series' such as *Unwrapped* and *Rachel Ray's Tasty Travels*. It also made the news as the backdrop of a protest during the 2008 Republican National Convention.

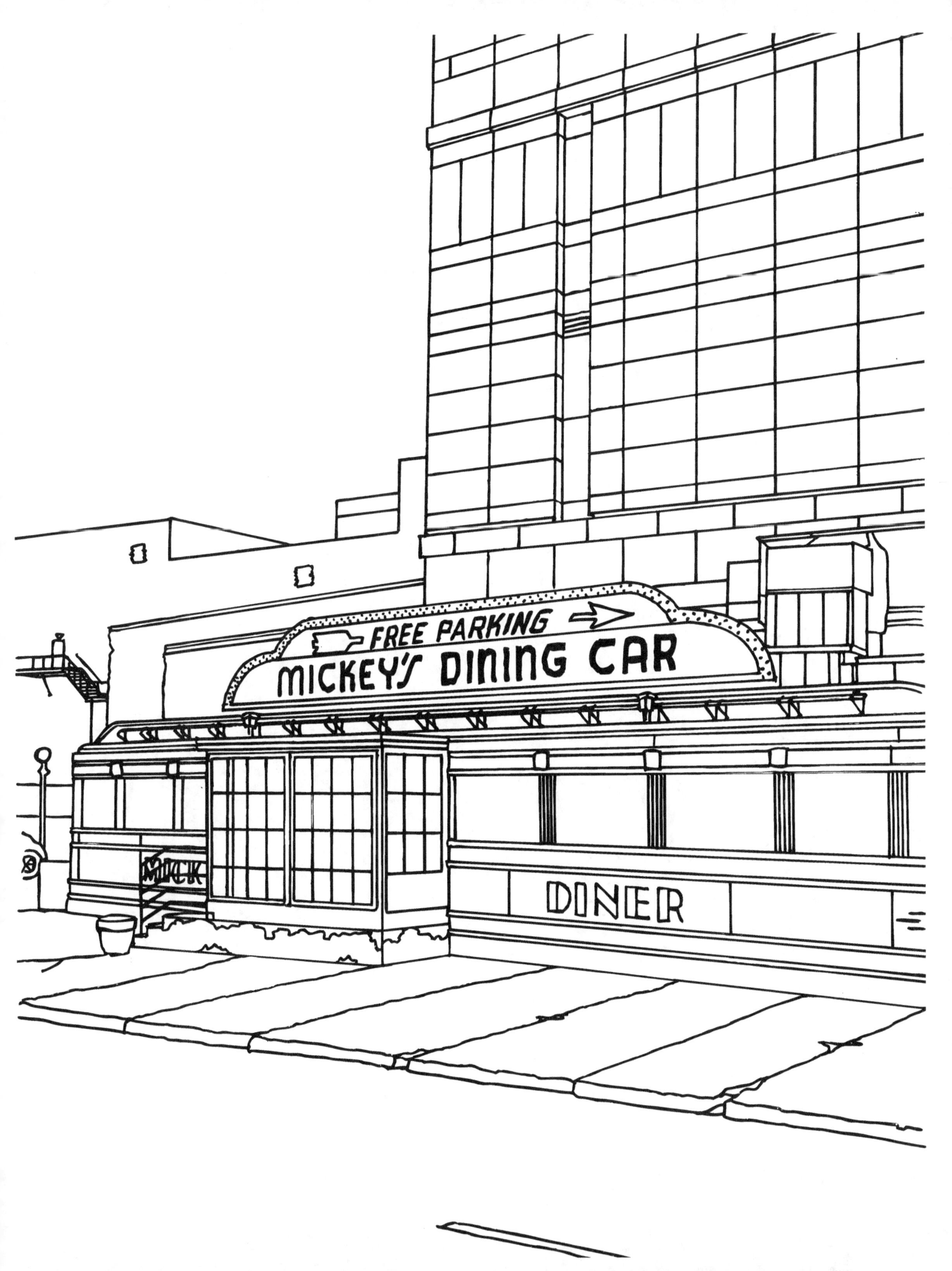

FREE PARKING
MICKEY'S DINING CAR
DINER

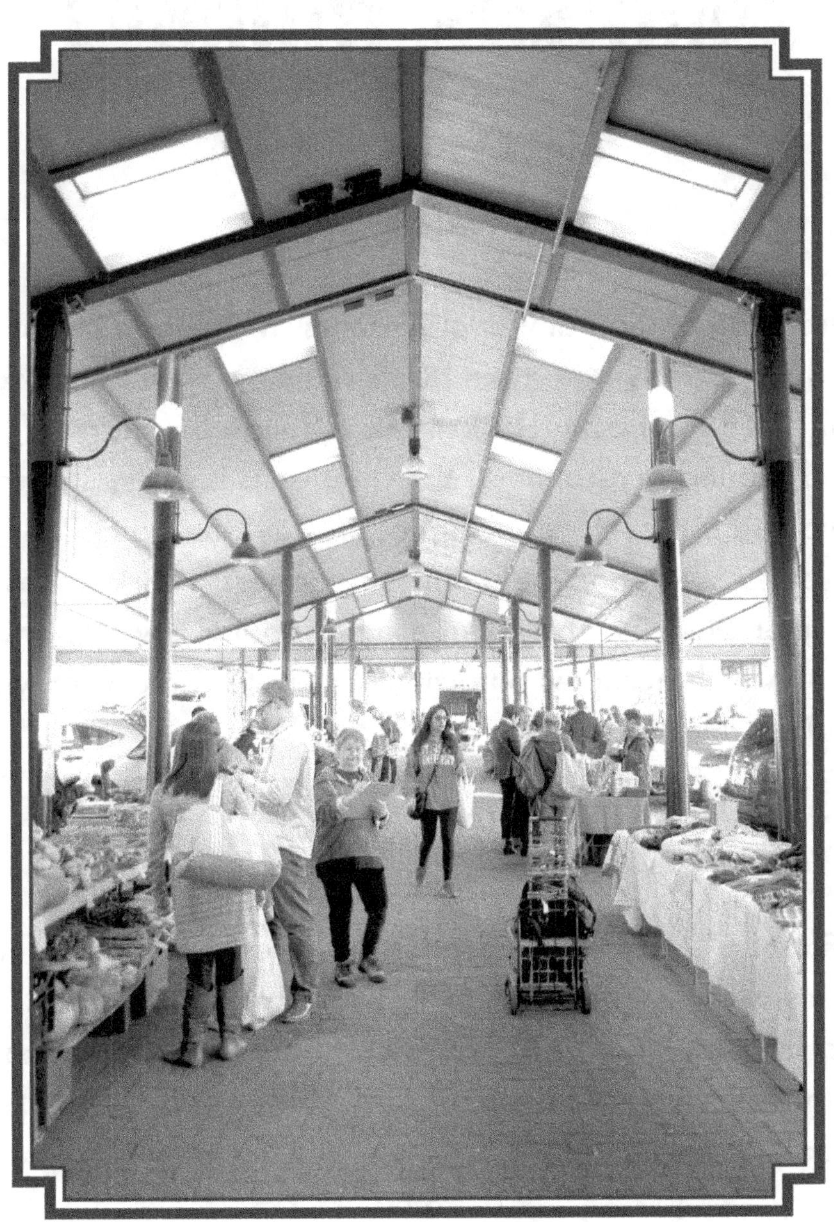

SAINT PAUL FARMERS' MARKET

- 1982 -

290 East 5th Street

The tradition of the Saint Paul Farmers' Market began in the 1850s, back when steamboats rules the rivers and log cabins lined the packed-dirt streets. Though the market moved around several times throughout its history, it always maintained a downtown presence. Today, the Saint Paul Growers' Association maintains 18 Farmers' Market sites throughout the city. This includes the popular Lowertown market, which occupies one city block between downtown Saint Paul and the river.

– FUN FACT –

The Farmers' Market offers more than fresh produce; meats, cheeses, syrups, eggs, honey, flowers, and baked goods can also be purchased here. Market hours are maintained throughout summer and winter, and some hearty vendors sell outdoors all year 'round.

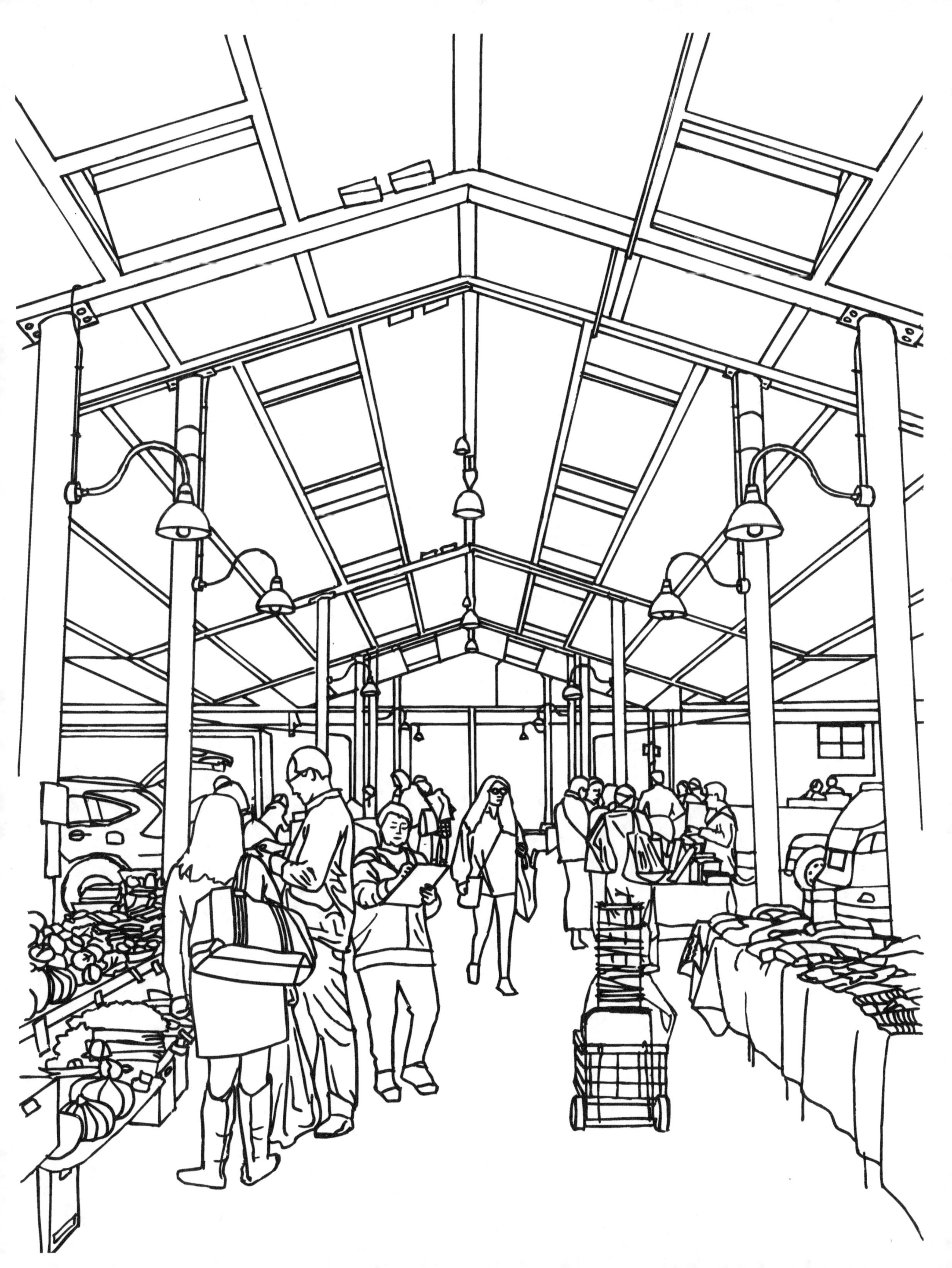

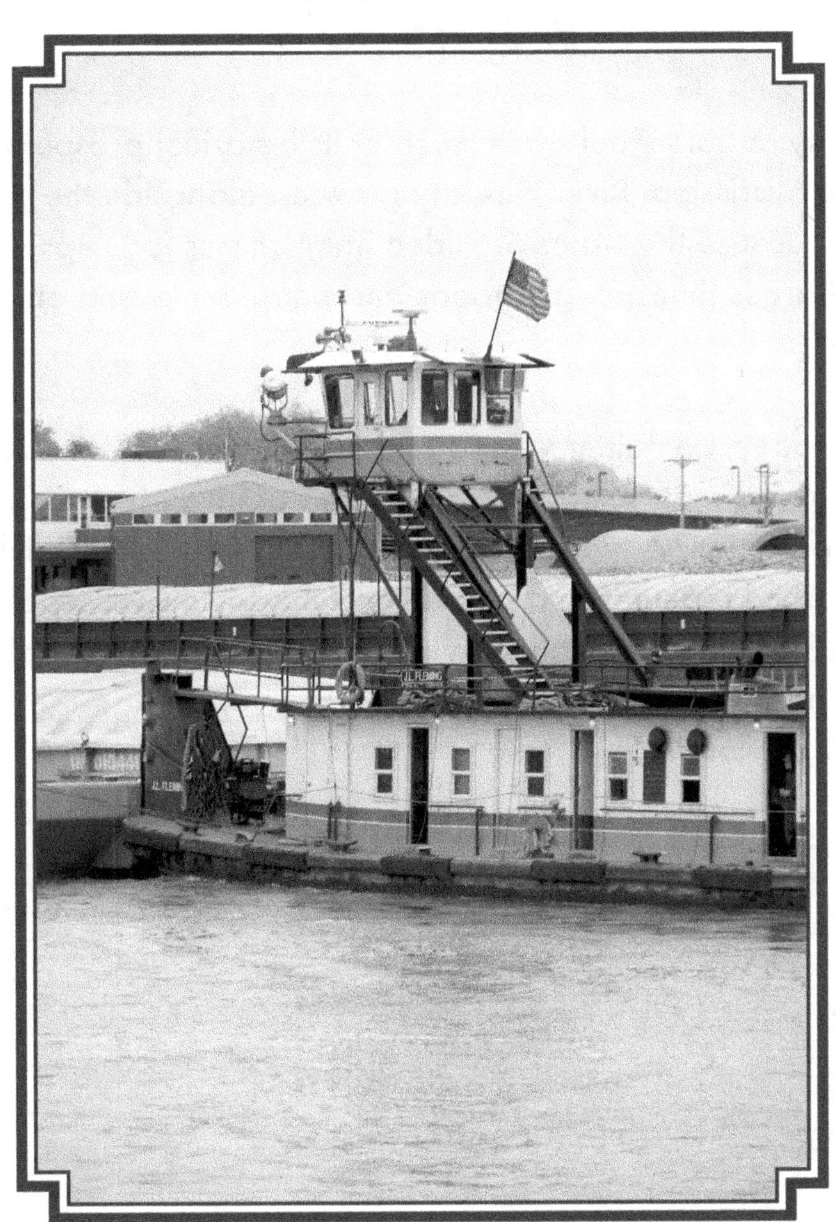

MISSISSIPPI RIVER BARGES

The city of Saint Paul owes much of its historical prosperity to the Mississippi River. The city grew up alongside the great river because the water provided easy access for ships and barges that brought goods and people into and out of the area.

Even today, container vessels and barges are still considered the top two most energy-efficient forms of large-scale transportation. A typical haul consists of 15 barges, which are lashed together and pushed up and down river by a tug boat. This total assembly may extend nearly a quarter of a mile in length, and haul the equivalent of 870 large semi-truck loads.

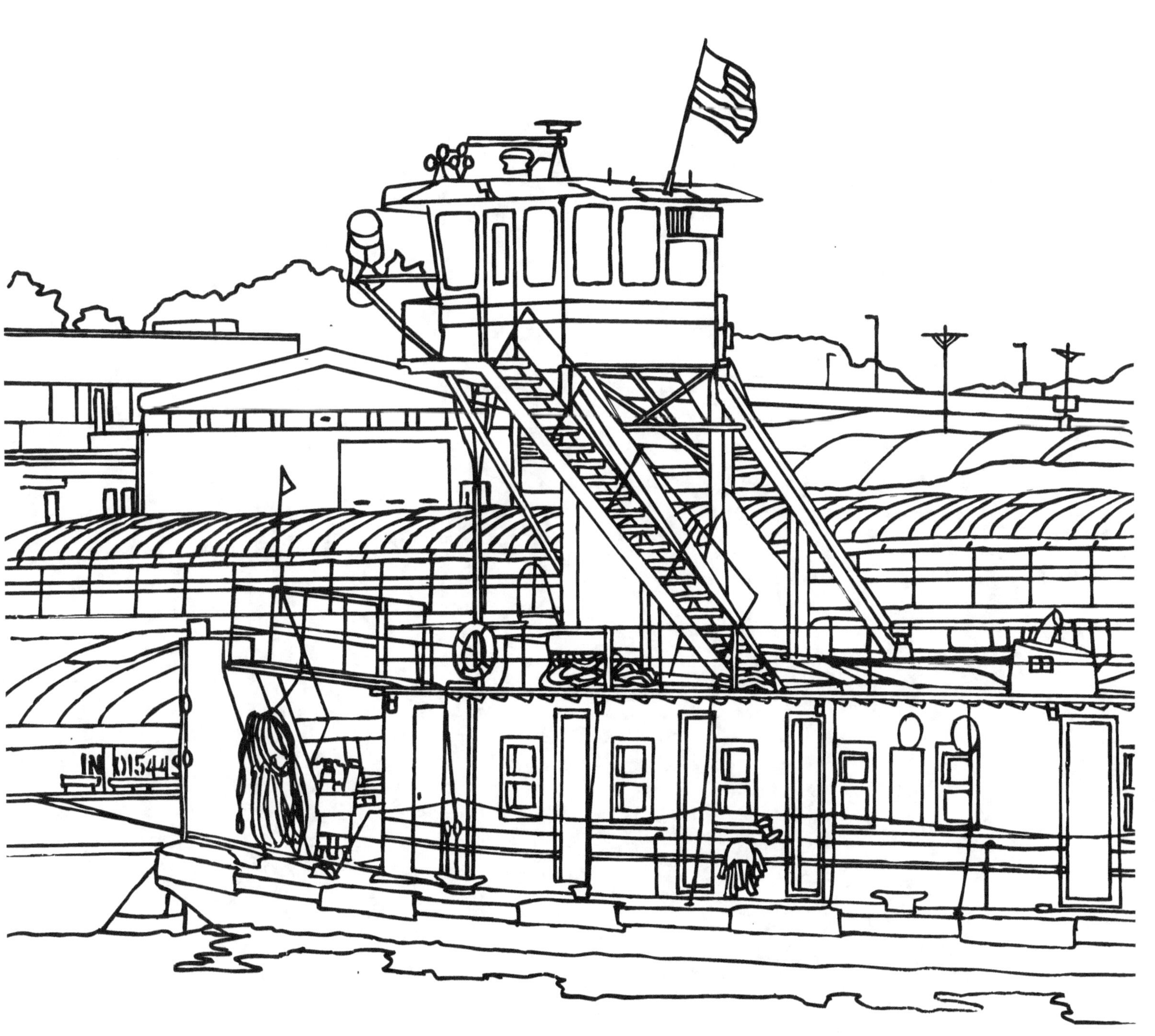
IN 1015449

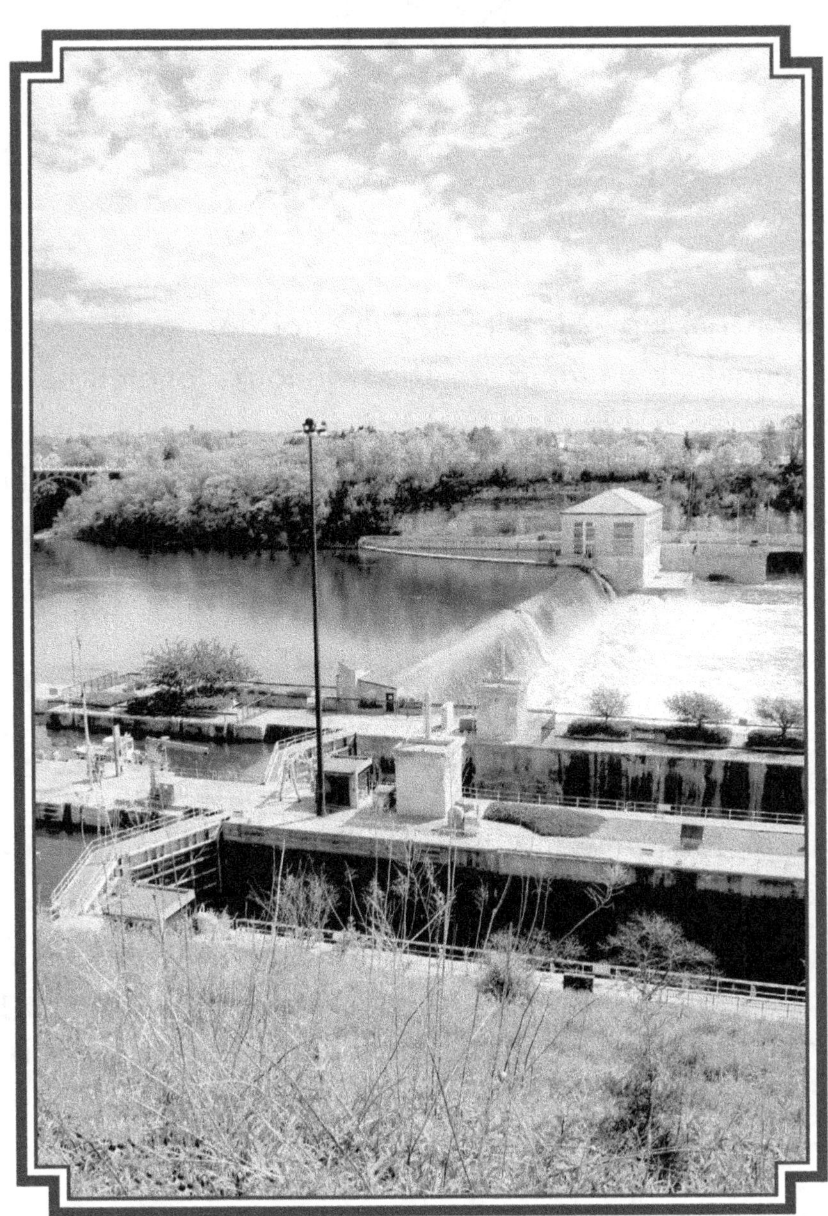

LOCK AND DAM NO. 1

- 1917 -

5000 West River Parkway

Lock and Dam No. 1 is currently the northernmost operational lock on the river. The twin locks located here accommodate a 39-foot difference in water level between Pool 1 (up-river) and Pool 2 (down-river). Commercial ships and personal watercraft can all use these locks to traverse the river.

- FUN FACT -

The dam alongside these locks was previously owned by Ford Motor Company, and was used to generate hydroelectric power for the nearby Twin Cities Assembly Plant. In 2007, the power station was sold to Brookfield Power Co., and is now used to feed the regional power grid. The water generates 14.4 megawatts of electricity. This is roughly enough energy to meet the power needs of 12,000 local residential homes.

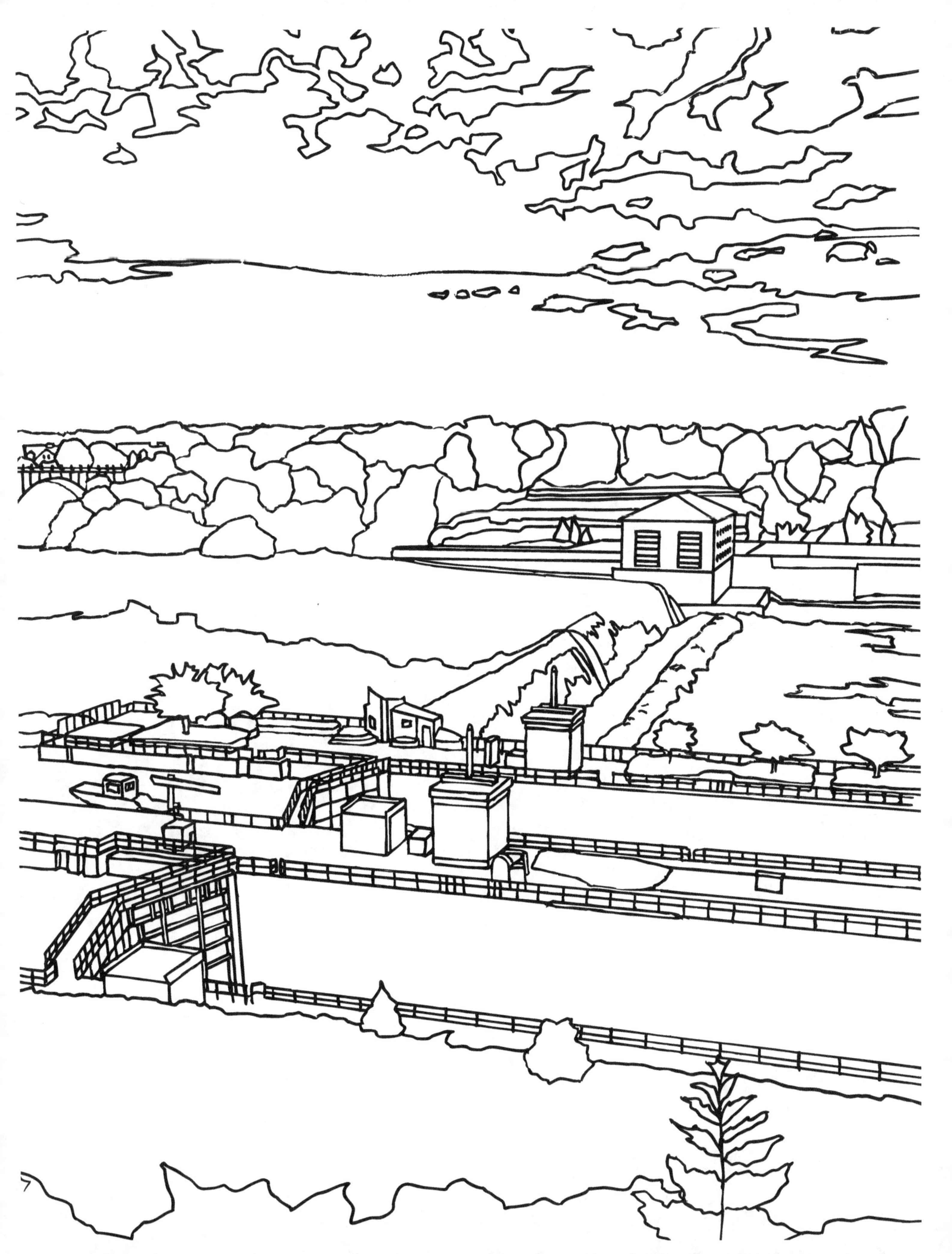

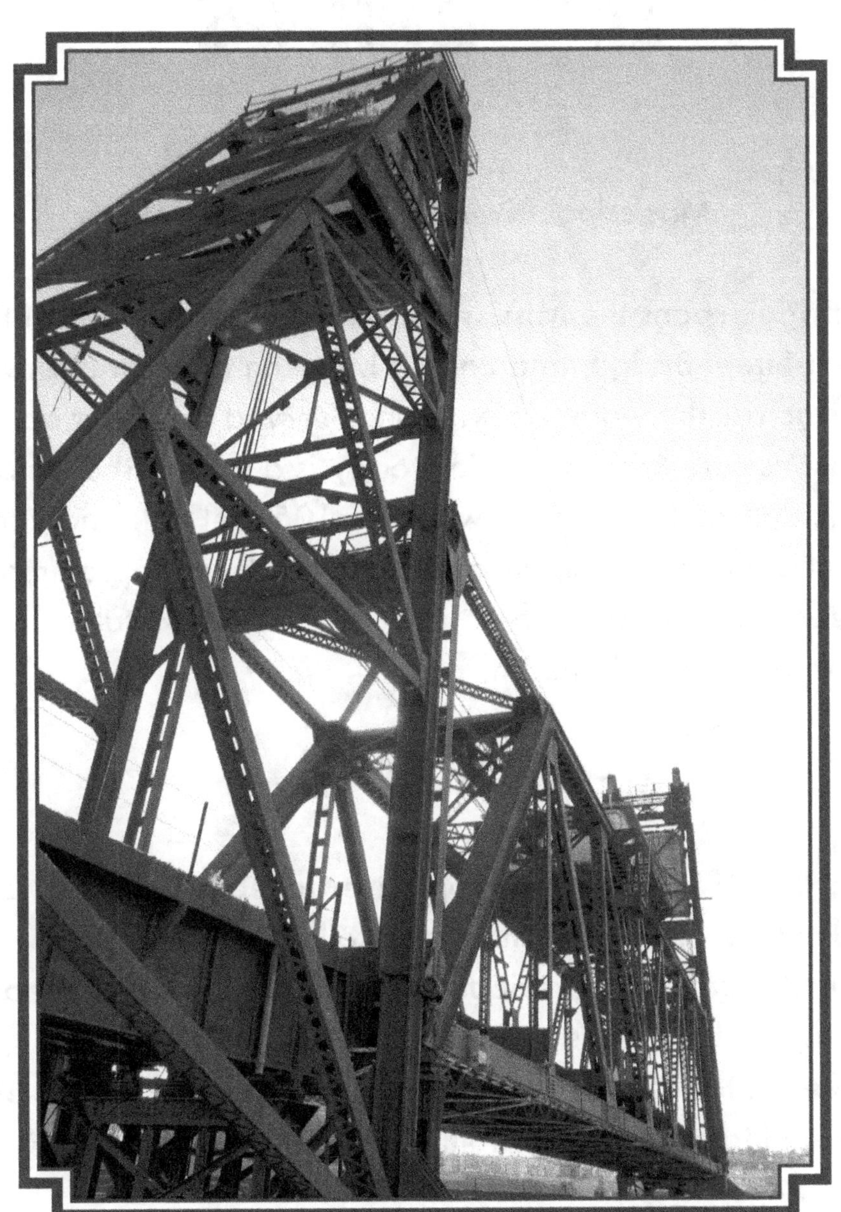

UNION PACIFIC LIFT BRIDGE

- 1913 -

Mississippi River, near Robert Street

This bridge spans the Mississippi River just to the west of the Robert Street Bridge, and carries between three and ten trains across the water daily. It once served the Chicago Great Western Railway, which today is a part of the Union Pacific Railroad. The two towers are 105 feet tall, and can raise the section of bridge between them from approximately 34 feet (lowered) to 72 feet (raised). This allows tall watercraft to pass beneath.

- FUN FACT -

In April of 1997, the Mississippi River faced one of the worst floods of the century. A snow-melt following a series of blizzards during the previous winter led to the simultaneous flooding of the Mississippi River and two of its major tributaries, the Red and the Minnesota Rivers. Water levels were said to reach the bottom of the span of the Lift Bridge that spring.

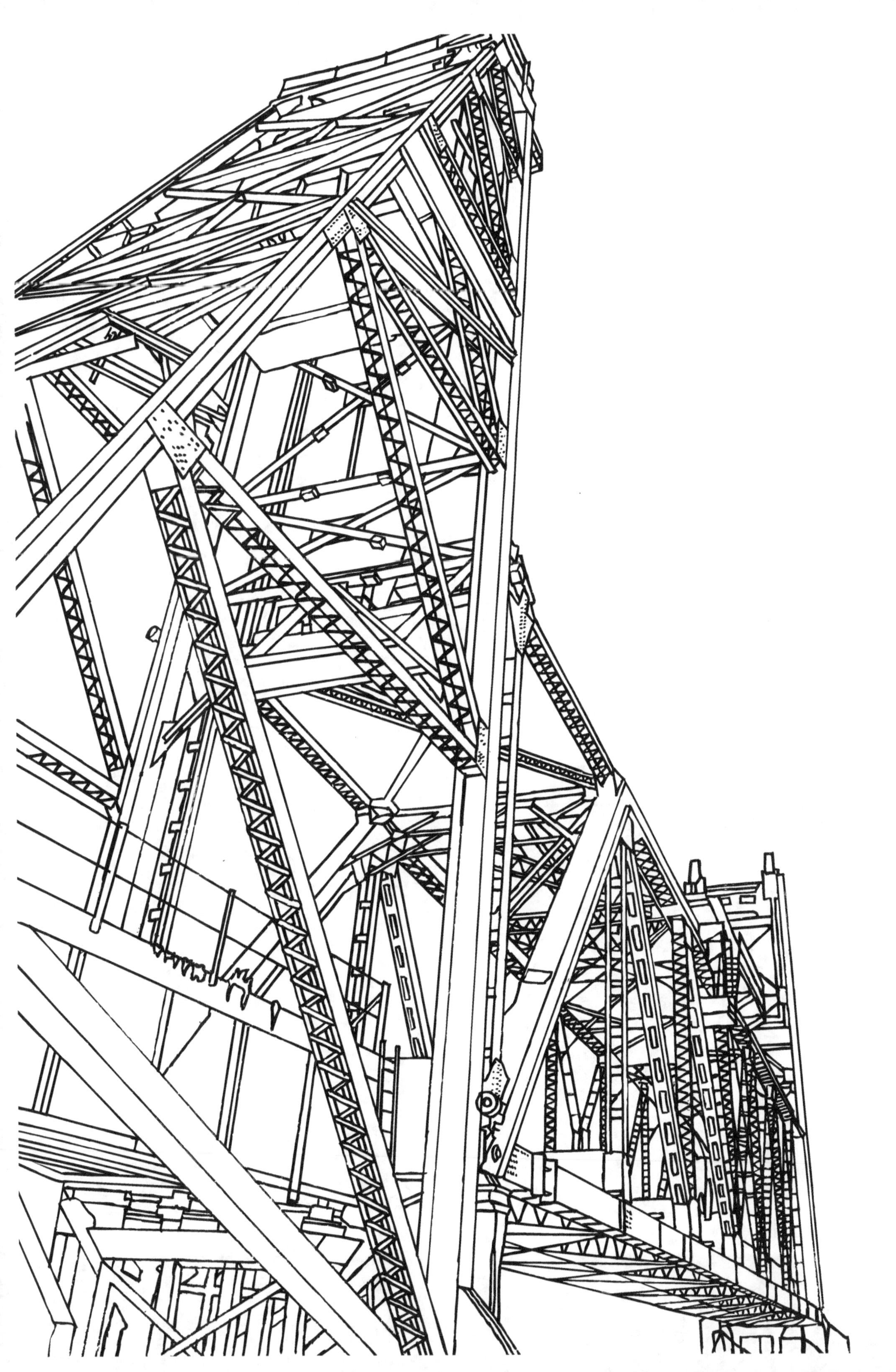

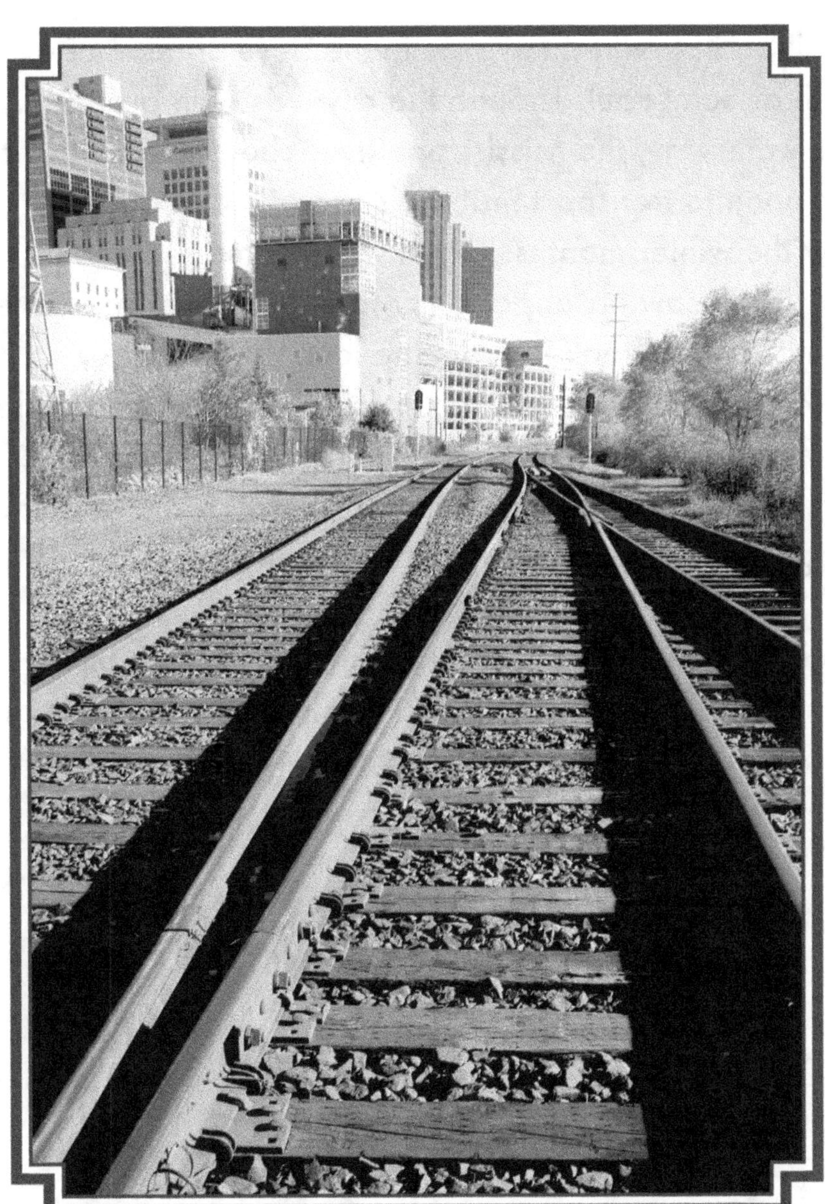

THE RAILROAD

The railroad played a key role in the development and growth of Saint Paul. Though the city was built around a major waterway, the Mississippi River could not always be relied upon to transport materials, goods, and people during the winter months. This is when "Empire Builder" James J. Hill saw his opportunity to expand the Midwestern railways, and he took it. From the late 1800s to the mid-1900s, Saint Paul was a hub for several major freight, mail, and passenger rail lines, including the Saint Paul & Pacific, the Great Northern, the Northern Pacific, and the Chicago Milwaukee Saint Paul and Pacific.

Though most of these historic rail lines have since been discontinued, sold, or merged, the railroad is still alive and well in Saint Paul today, and continues to serve the city's backbone industries.

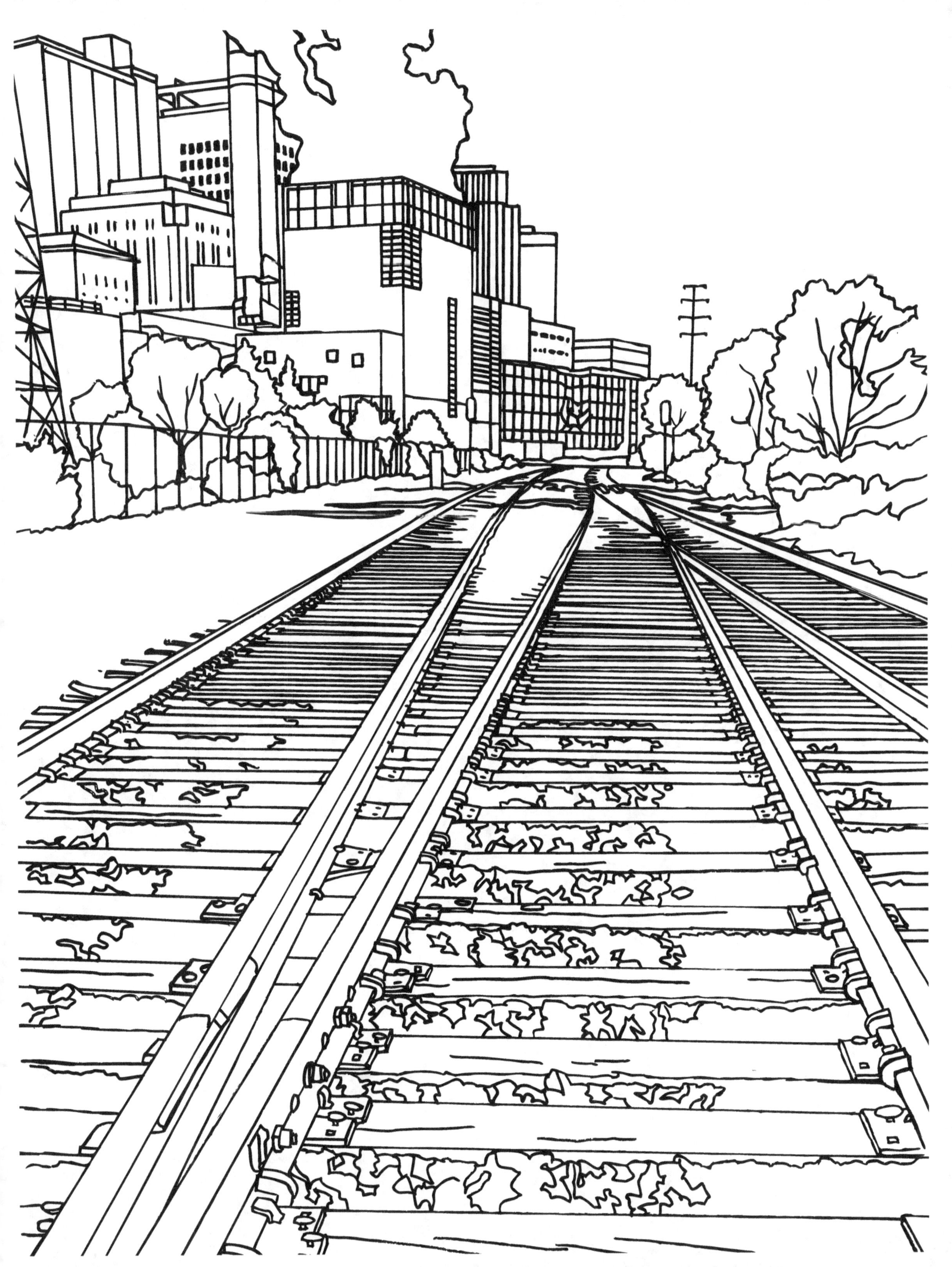

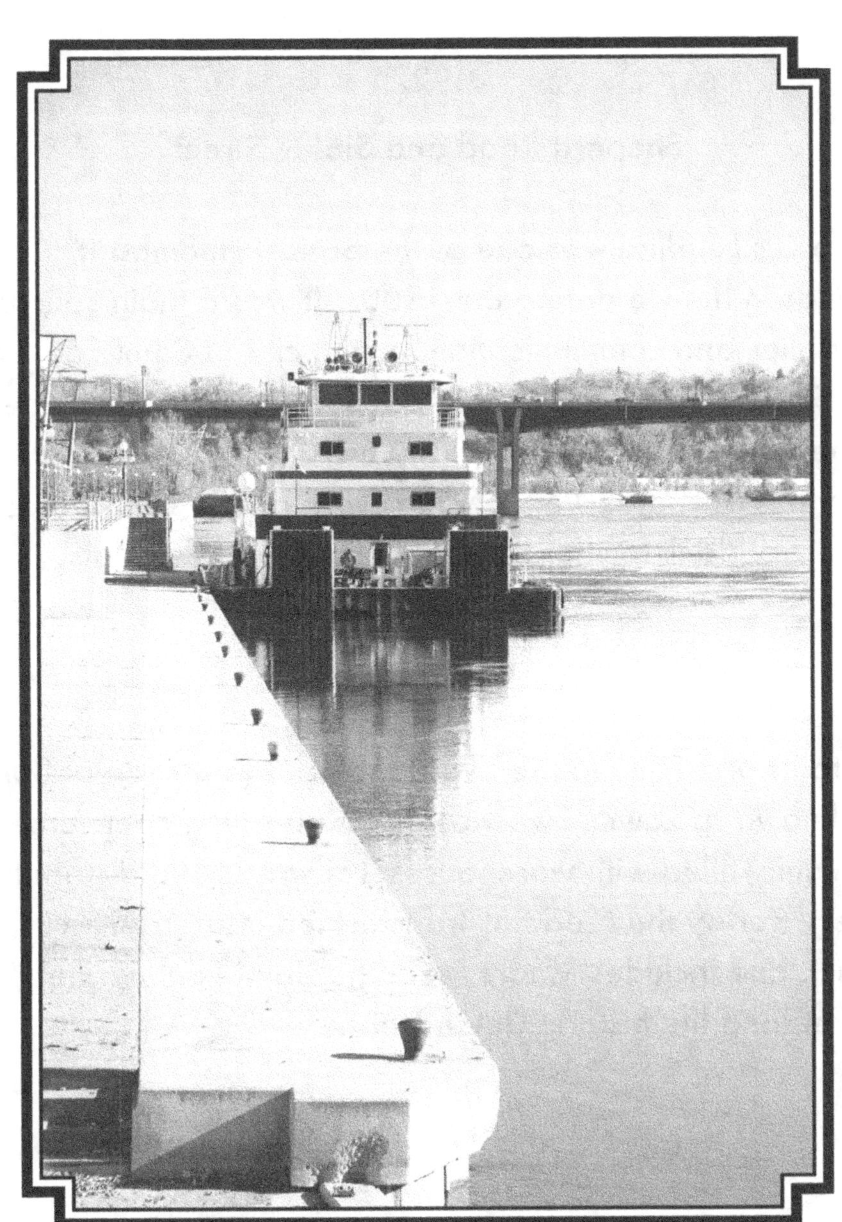

LAMBERT'S LANDING

- 1927 -

Shepard Road and Sibley Street

The Lower Landing was one of the busiest steamboat landings in the US during the 1800s. It was a main source of supplies and communication for the city of Saint Paul until the railroad era began in the 1880s. In 1937 it was named Lambert's Landing as part of a riverfront revival project. Today it is part of Lower Landing Park, and is still used as a temporary dock for barges and historic paddle boats.

- FUN FACT -

Due to its proximity to the river landing, the section of Saint Paul known as Lowertown was once a bustling commerce community filled with warehouses, railways, and distribution centers. Today the area has transformed into an Artist District, and includes Mears Park, the Saint Paul Farmers' Market, and the historic Union Depot.

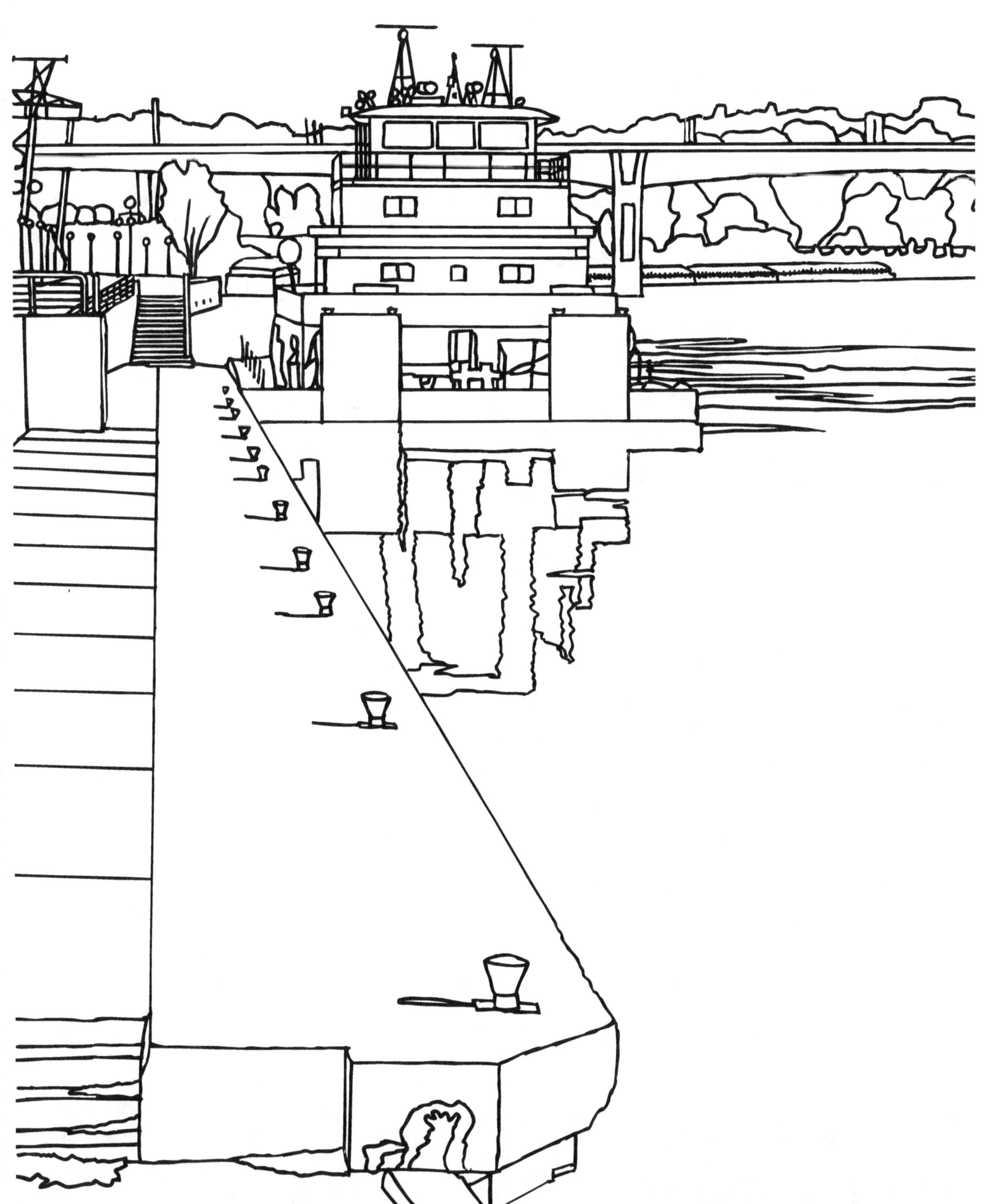

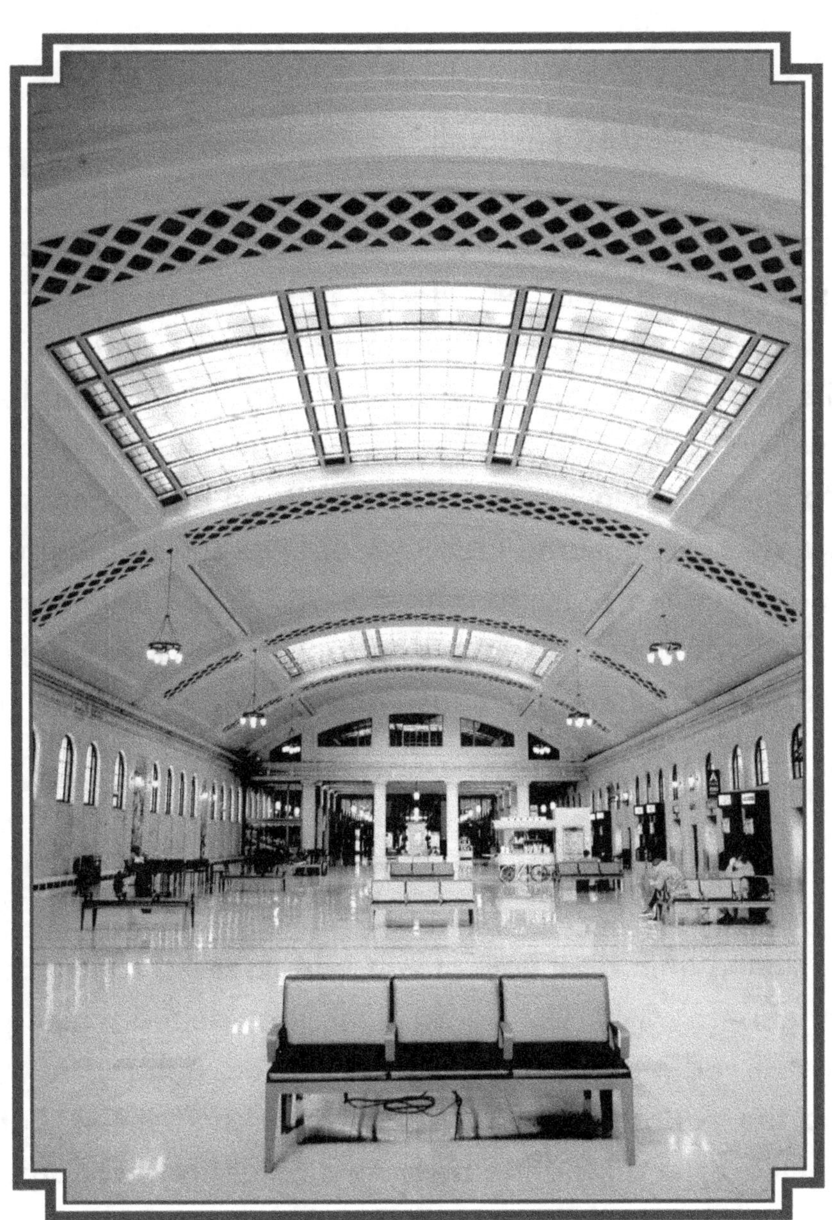

UNION DEPOT

- 1923 -

240 East Kellogg Boulevard

This neoclassical building was commissioned by railroad baron James J. Hill and was designed by architect Charles Forst. It was the grand entrance to the city of Saint Paul, and its 10 platforms and 21 passenger tracks once bustled with activity. Over the years, rail travel tapered off until the station closed in 1971. The Depot stood empty for several decades until the Ramsey County Regional Railroad Authority initiated plans to renovate and reopen the station in 2005. Today Union Depot is not only a transportation hub, but also a setting for public and private events, cultural festivals, and concerts.

- FUN FACT -

Many young men and women were deployed through Union Depot during WWII. During that time the vaulted waiting room's curved glass skylights were covered with tar to protect the troops from potential air attacks. These skylights were uncovered during the building's recent renovations.

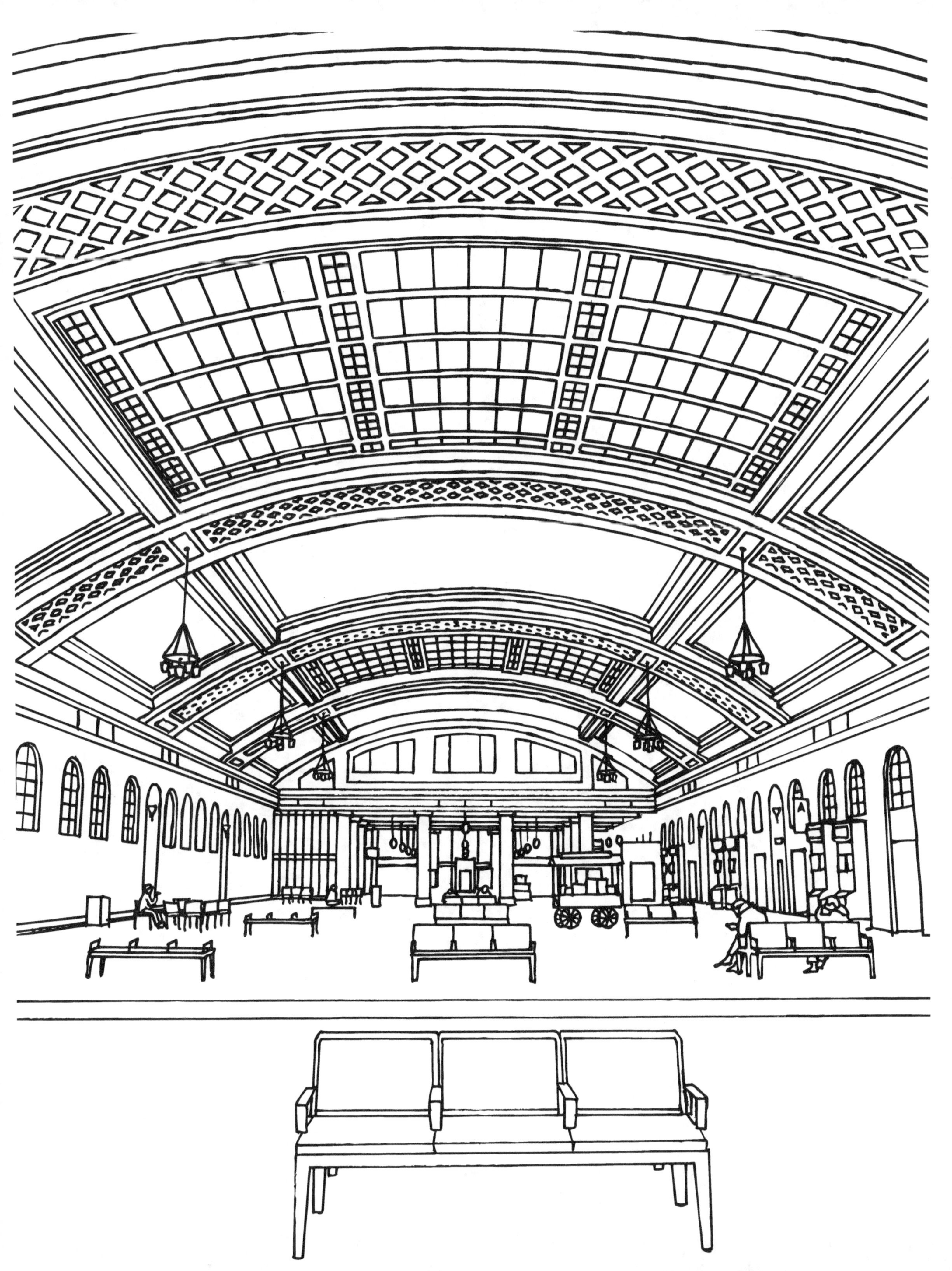

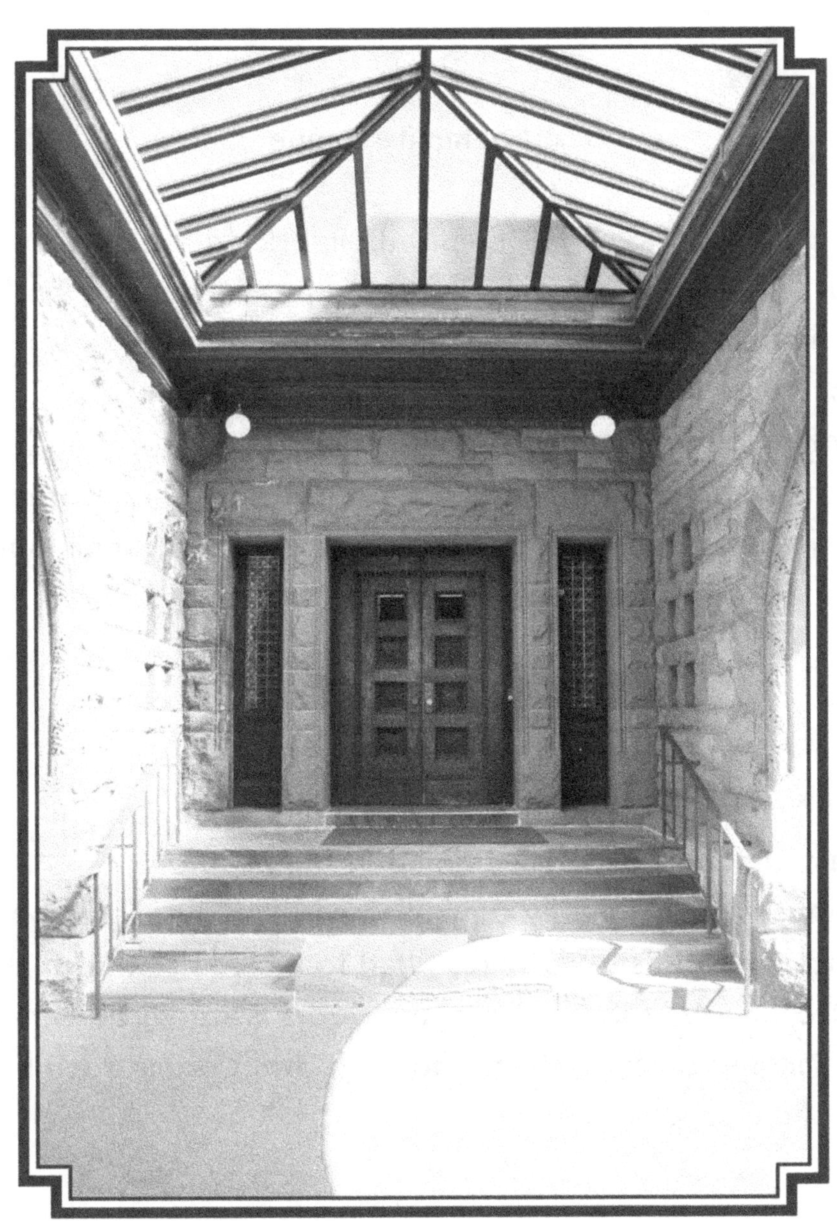

JAMES J. HILL HOUSE

- 1891 -

240 Summit Avenue

This house was home to "Empire Builder" railroad baron James J. Hill and his family. After the passing of Hill, and later his wife in 1921, the house changed hands several times. It was gifted to the Catholic Archdiocese of Saint Paul and served as an office building, school, and church residence until it was acquired by the Minnesota Historical Society in 1978. Today it is open for public tours and special events.

- FUN FACT -

At the time it was built, the James J. Hill House was the largest and most expensive home in Minnesota.
The house was originally equipped with the most advanced technologies of its day. It was fitted to include both gas and electric fixtures. The windows and doors were wired with a sophisticated alarm system, and its 13 bathrooms each had state-of-the-art plumbing.

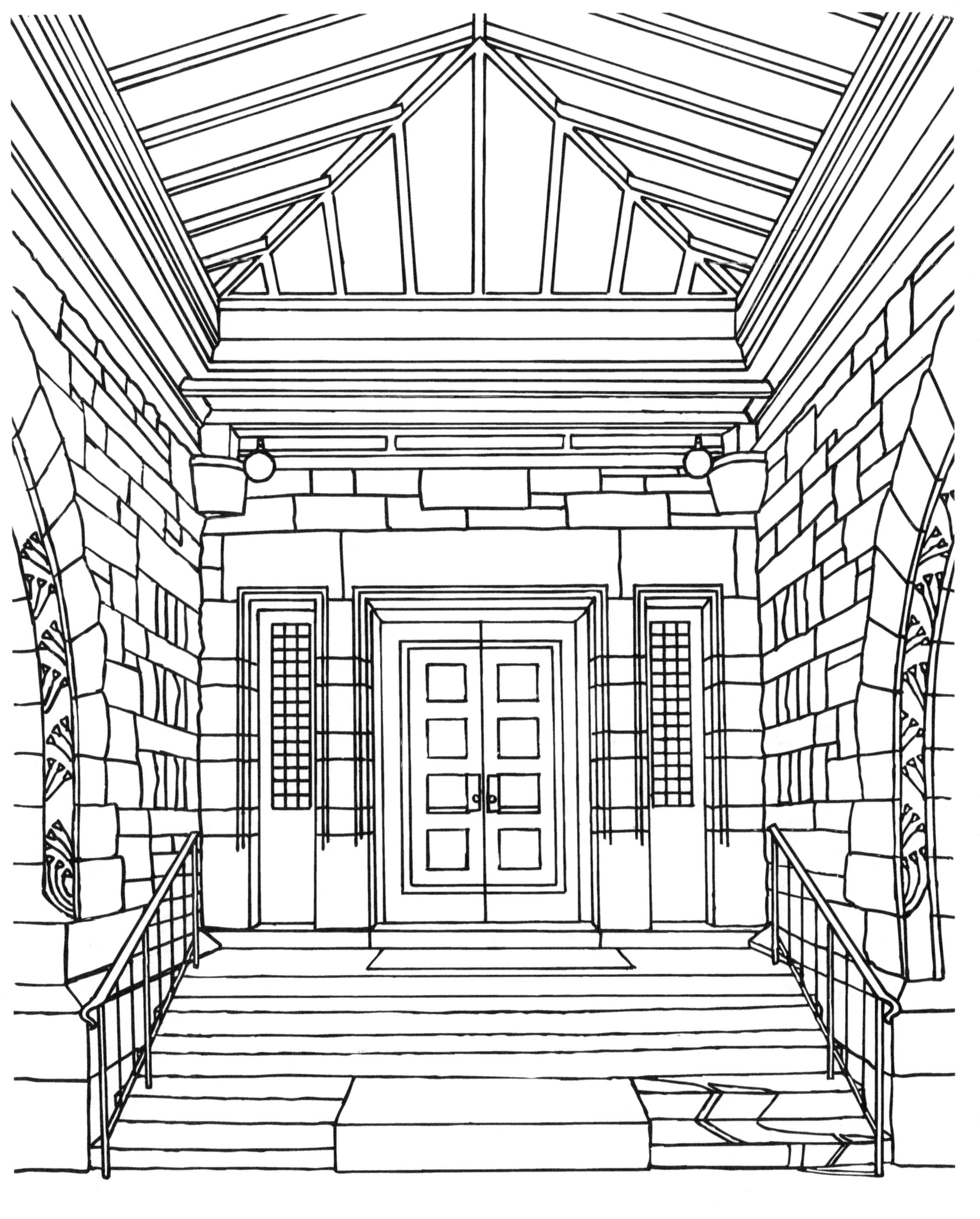

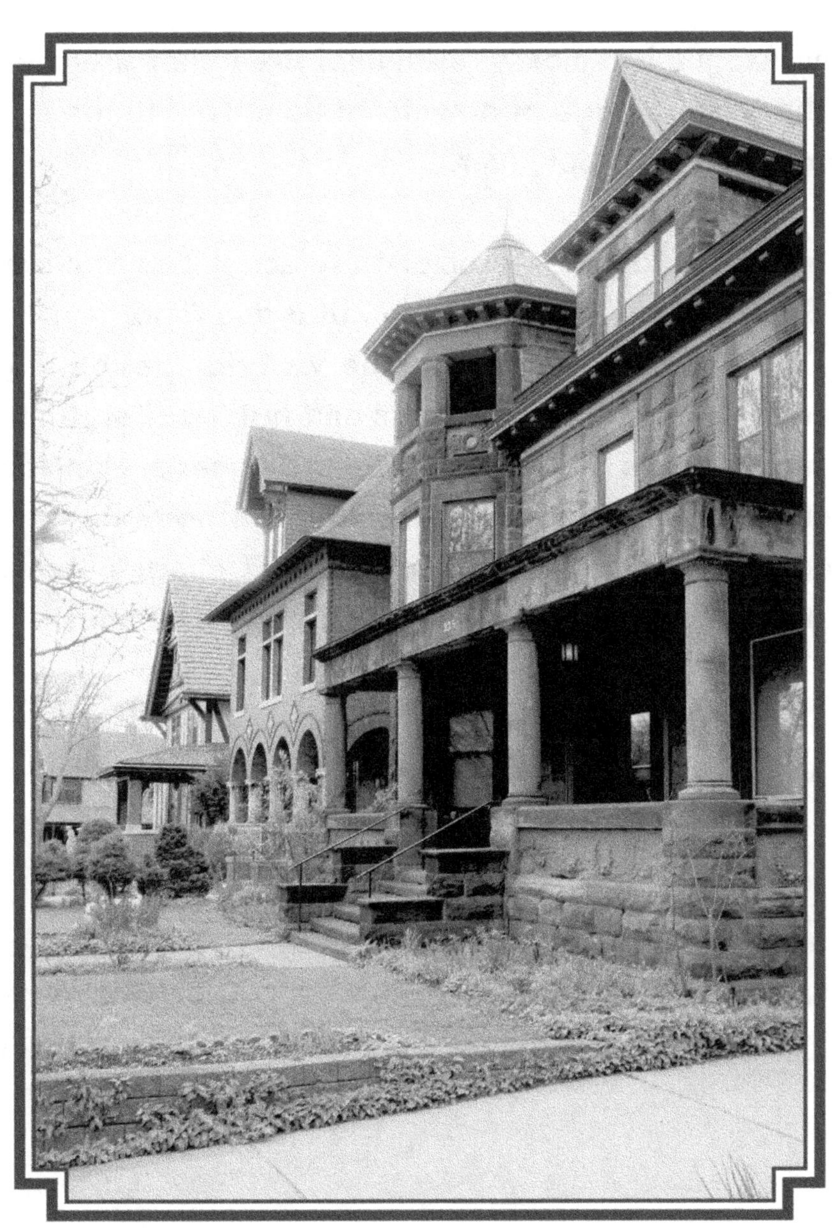

SUMMIT AVENUE

Summit Avenue is a mostly-residential street that stretches from the western edge of downtown Saint Paul to the eastern edge of the Mississippi River.

The American Planning Association selected it as one of the ten "Great Streets" in America in 2008 due to its well-preserved architecture from the Victorian period. It is known for its abundance of iconic and historic sites. Some of its most notable buildings include the James J. Hill House, F. Scott Fitzgerald House, Minnesota Governor's Residence, Cathedral of Saint Paul, William Mitchell College of Law, Macalester College, and the University of St. Thomas.

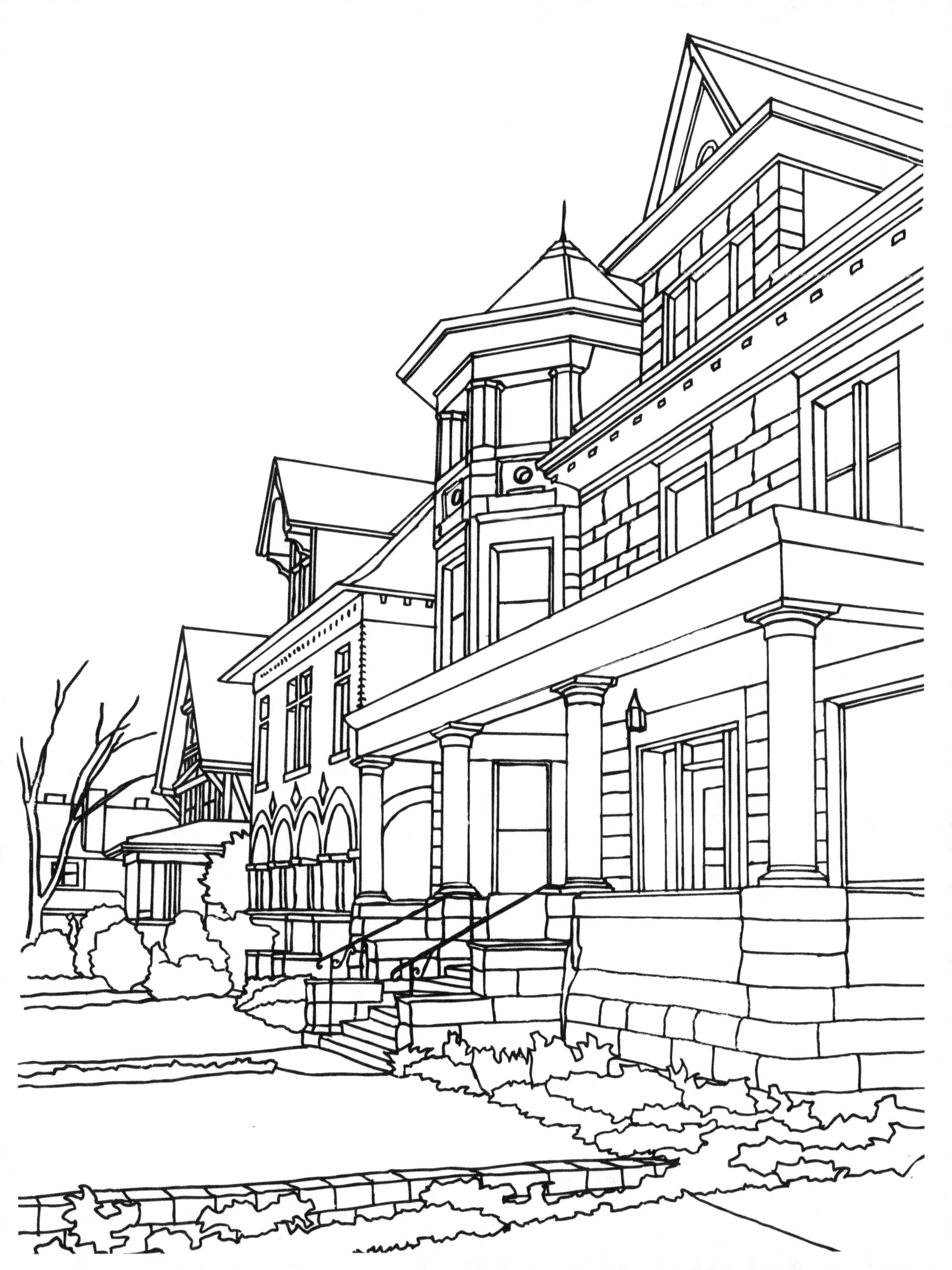

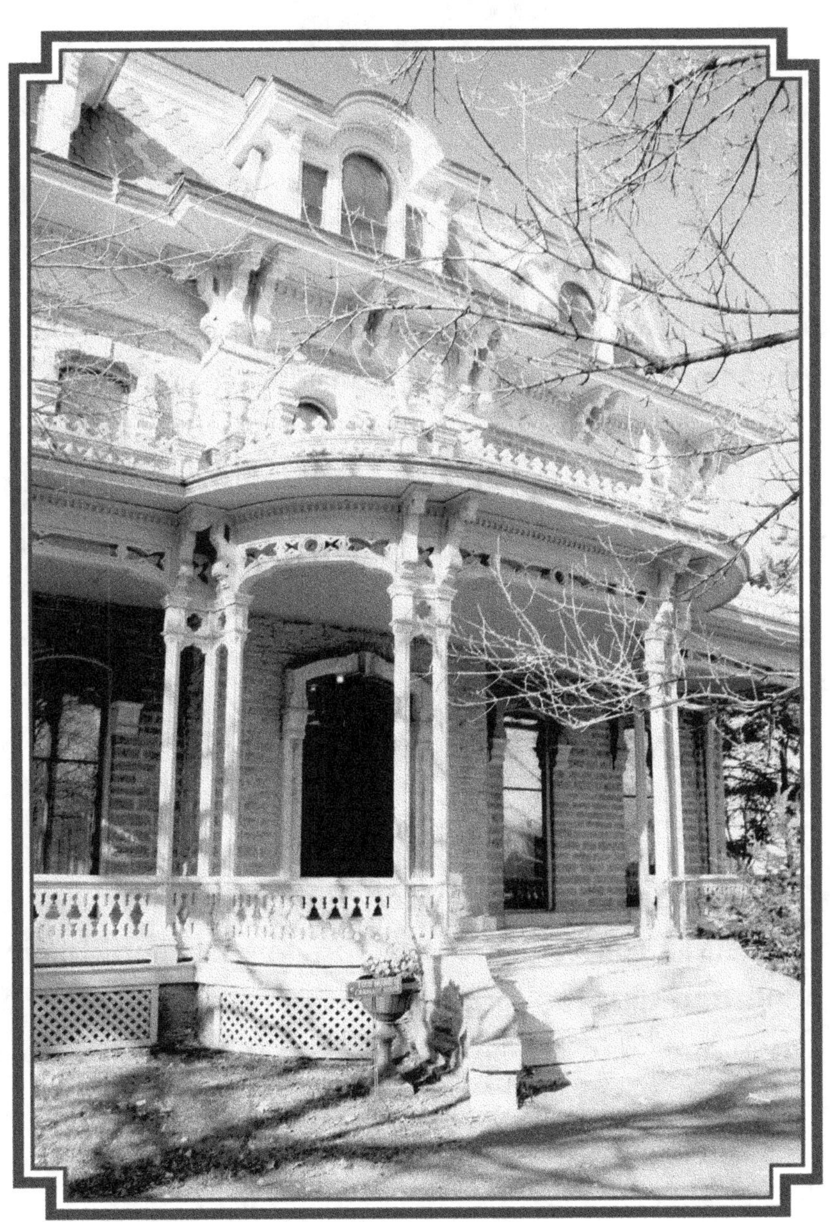

ALEXANDER RAMSEY HOUSE

- 1872 -

265 South Exchange Street

Alexander Ramsey was the first territorial governor of Minnesota in 1848. His house is considered one of the nation's best preserved houses from the Victorian era. It remained in the family until the death of his last surviving granddaughter in 1964. At that time the house and property were left to the Minnesota Historical Society. It's now open for public tours and special programs.

- FUN FACT -

A Victorian Christmas at the Ramsey House is one of the house's biggest events of the year. During the holiday season, its main rooms are decorated with original family ornaments and gifts, holiday music is played on the 1875 Steinway piano, and cookies are baked in the wood stove.

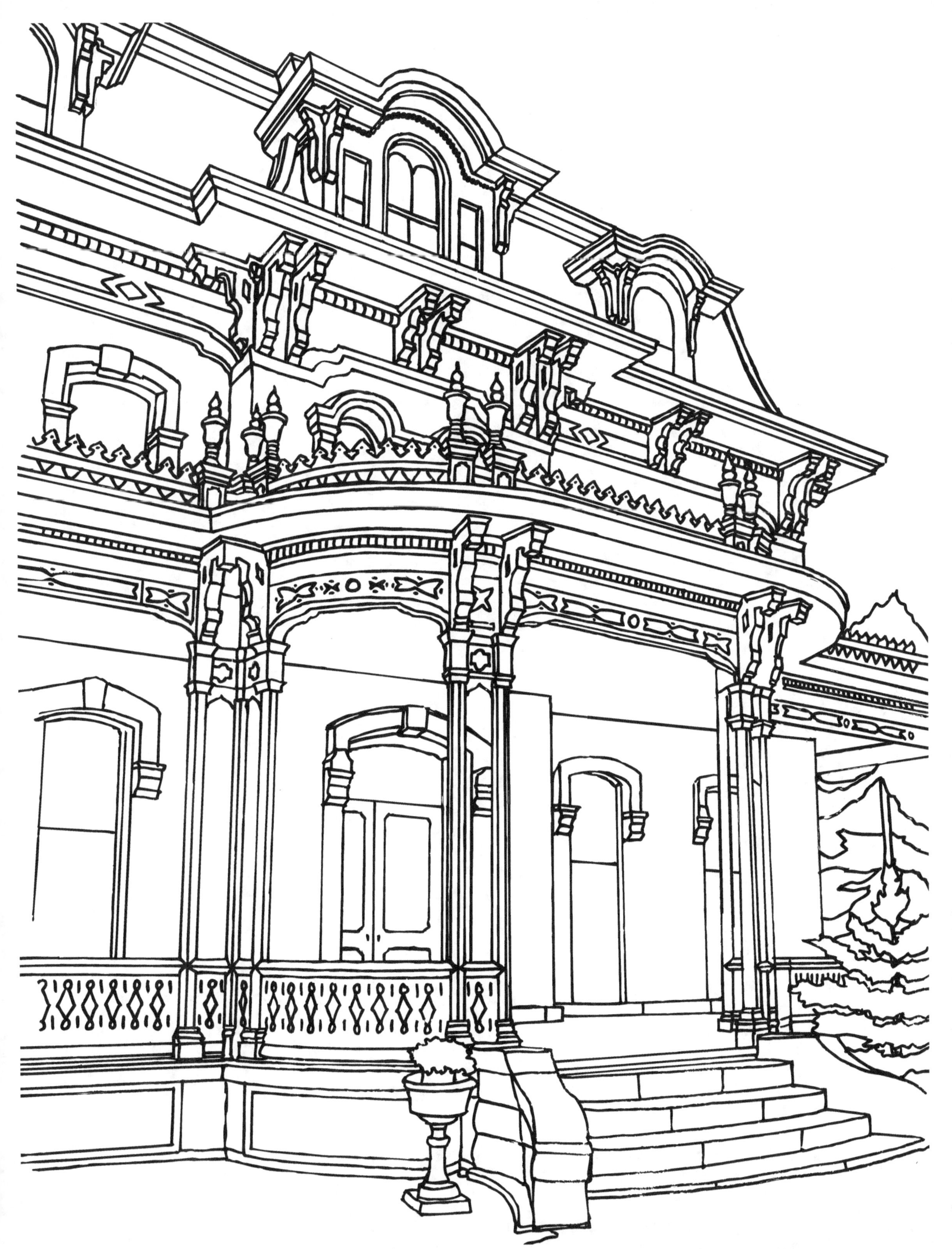

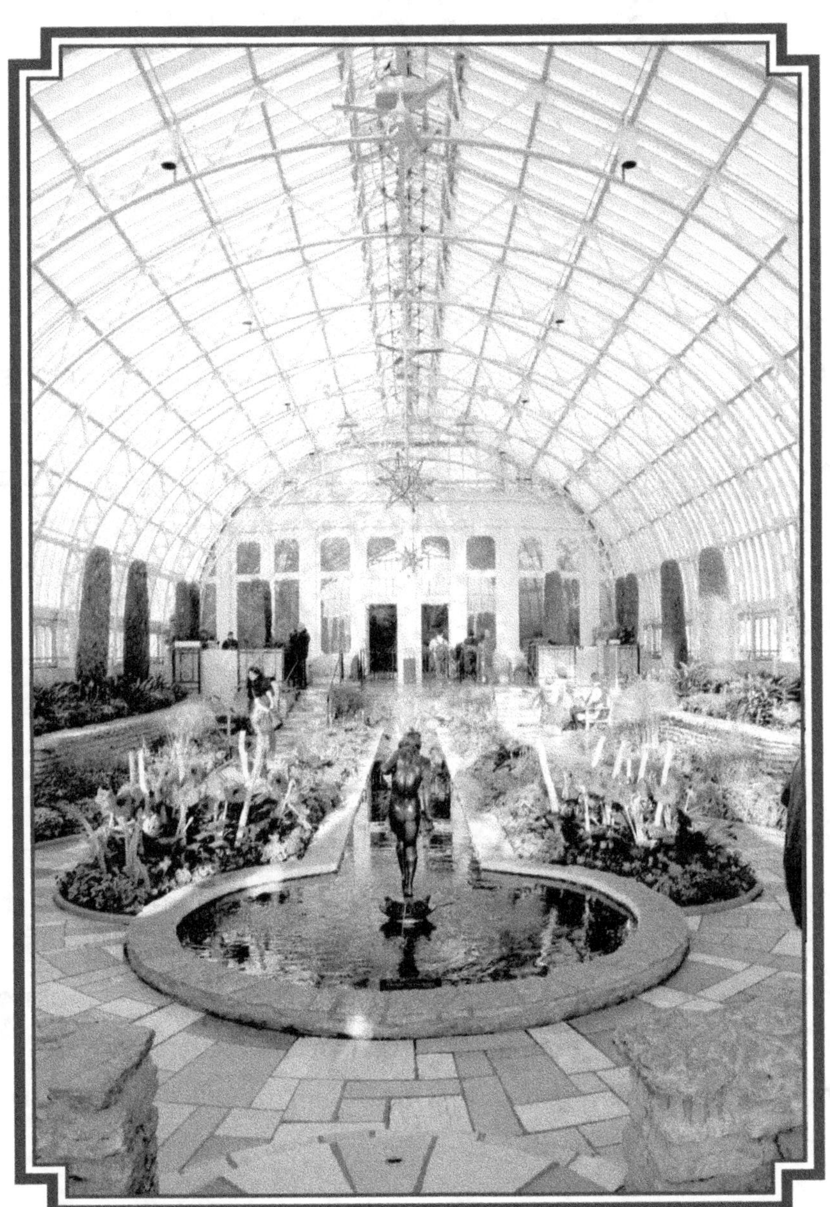

MARJORIE MCNEELY CONSERVATORY

- 1915 -

1225 Estabrook Drive

The Marjorie McNeely Conservatory is a collection of gardens: three of them outdoors, and six of them enclosed within a one-acre glass expanse. It is part of a larger group of attractions in northeast Saint Paul that also includes Como Park Zoo, Lake Como, an amusement park, a carousel, and a golf course. The Conservatory is open all year, and admission is free.

- FUN FACT -

A number of rare and unusual plants inhabit the Conservatory, one of the more notable of which is the Amorphophallus titanum. It is commonly known as the Corpse Flower, but it also goes by the affectionate nickname "Bob." This peculiar flower of Indonesian origin doesn't bloom often, but when it does (as it did in 2008), it emits a distinct odor of rotting flesh.

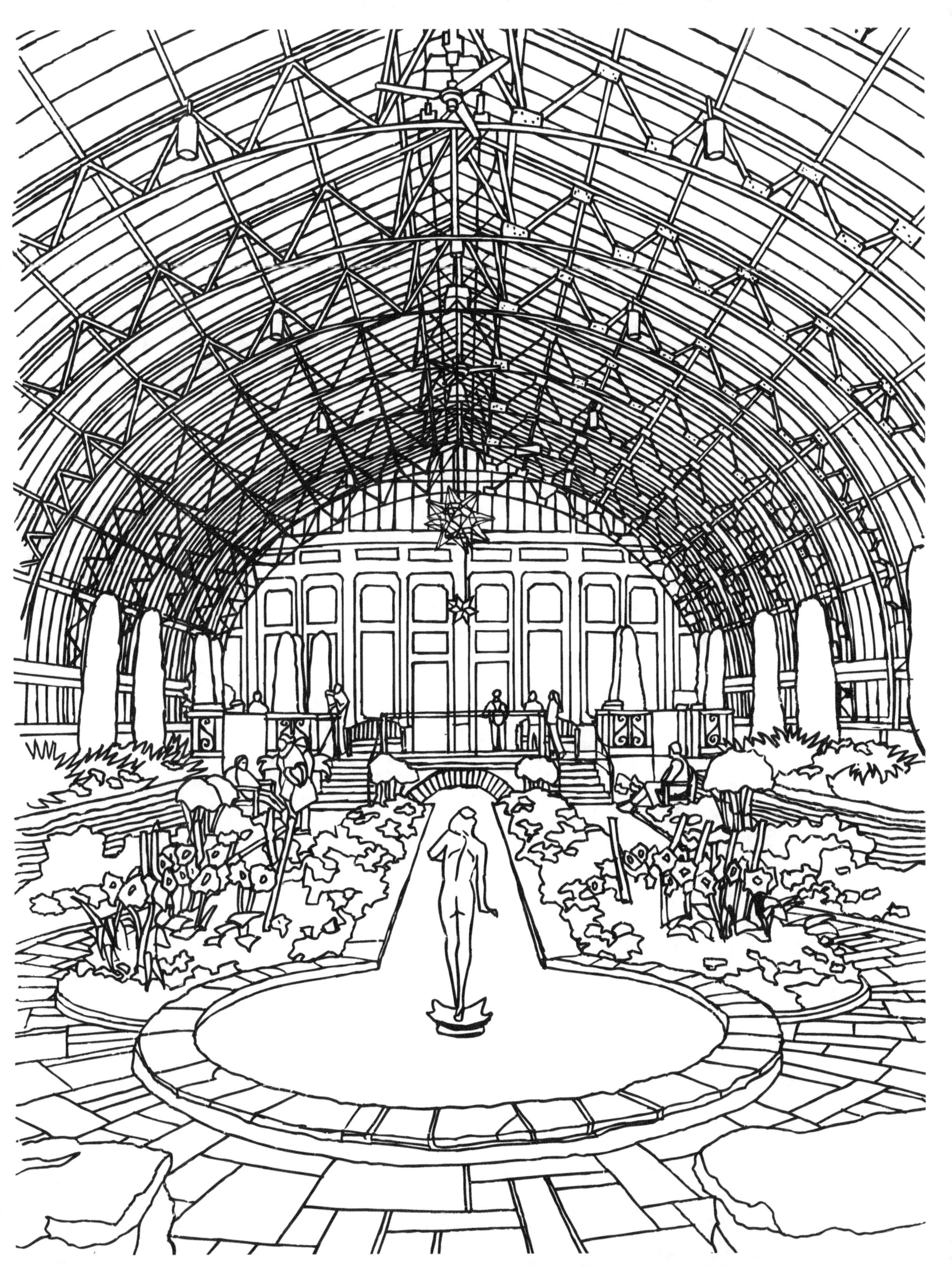

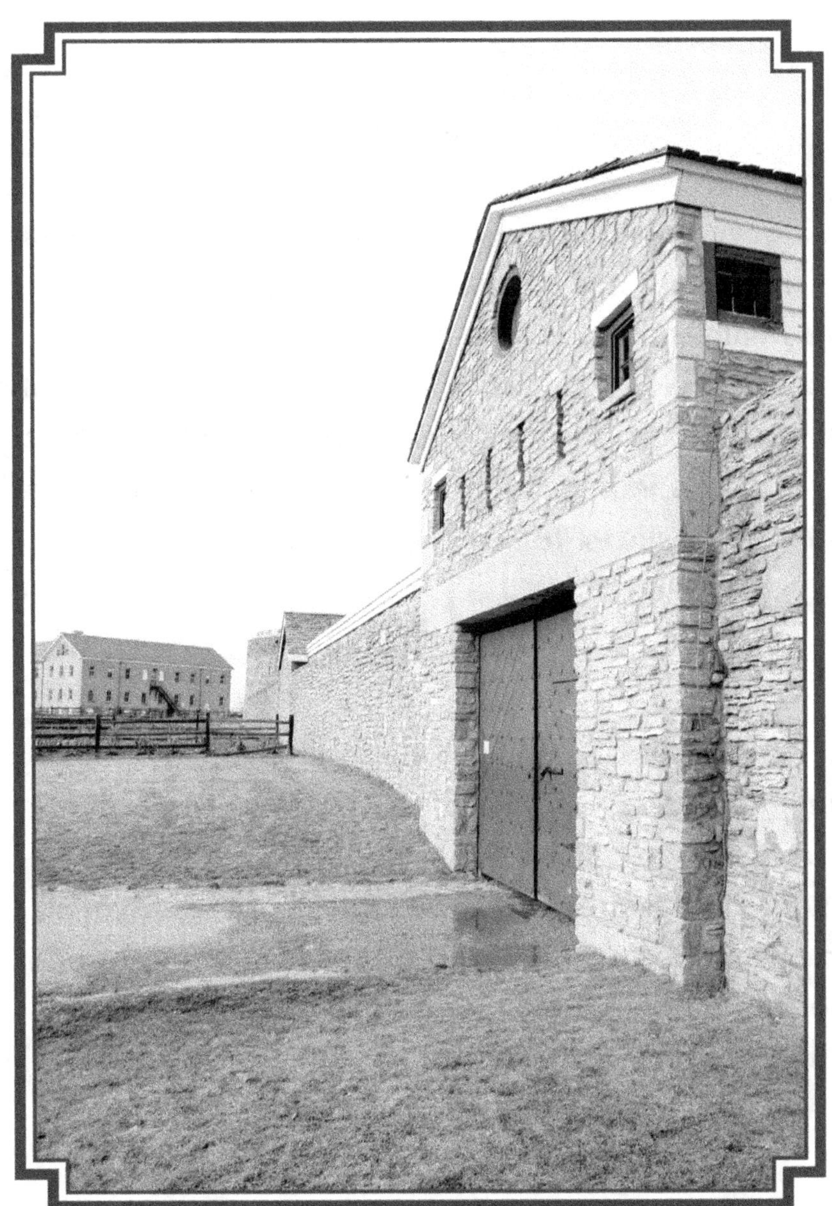

FORT SNELLING

- 1820s -

200 Tower Avenue

The US government established Fort Snelling at the juncture of the Mississippi and Minnesota Rivers several decades before Minnesota became a state. The fort served two main purposes: to promote and protect US interests in the lucrative fur trade, and to develop friendly relationships with local American Indian communities. This historic landmark is open to the public in the spring, summer, and fall.

- FUN FACT -

By the mid-1950s only four of the fort's original buildings remained standing, and the State Highway Department was proposing to build a freeway through the area. Archaeologists managed to save the site by excavating it and uncovering artifacts and original foundations too precious to be paved over. Over the course of several decades, the fort was painstakingly uncovered, researched, and reconstructed to its 1820s appearance.

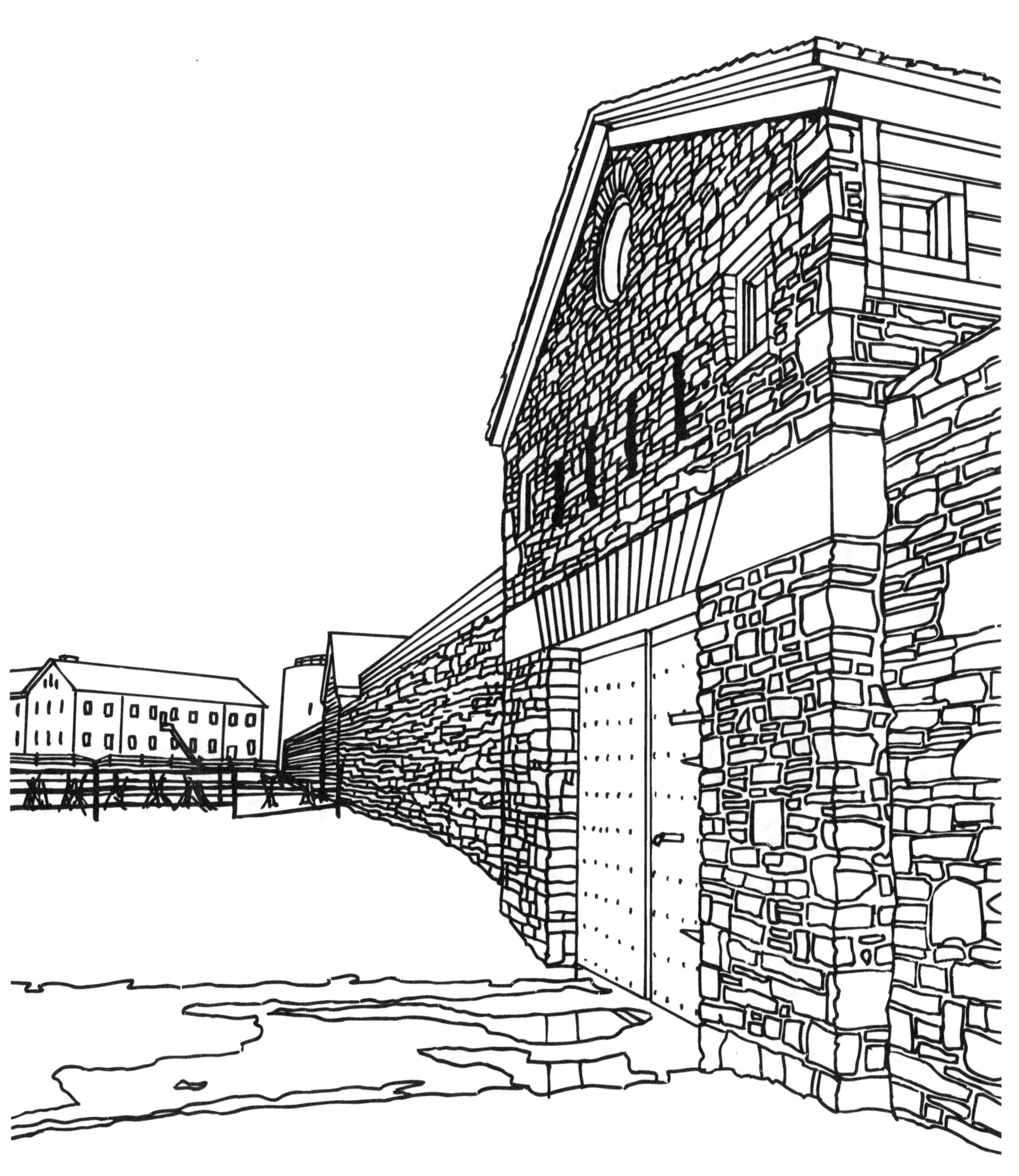

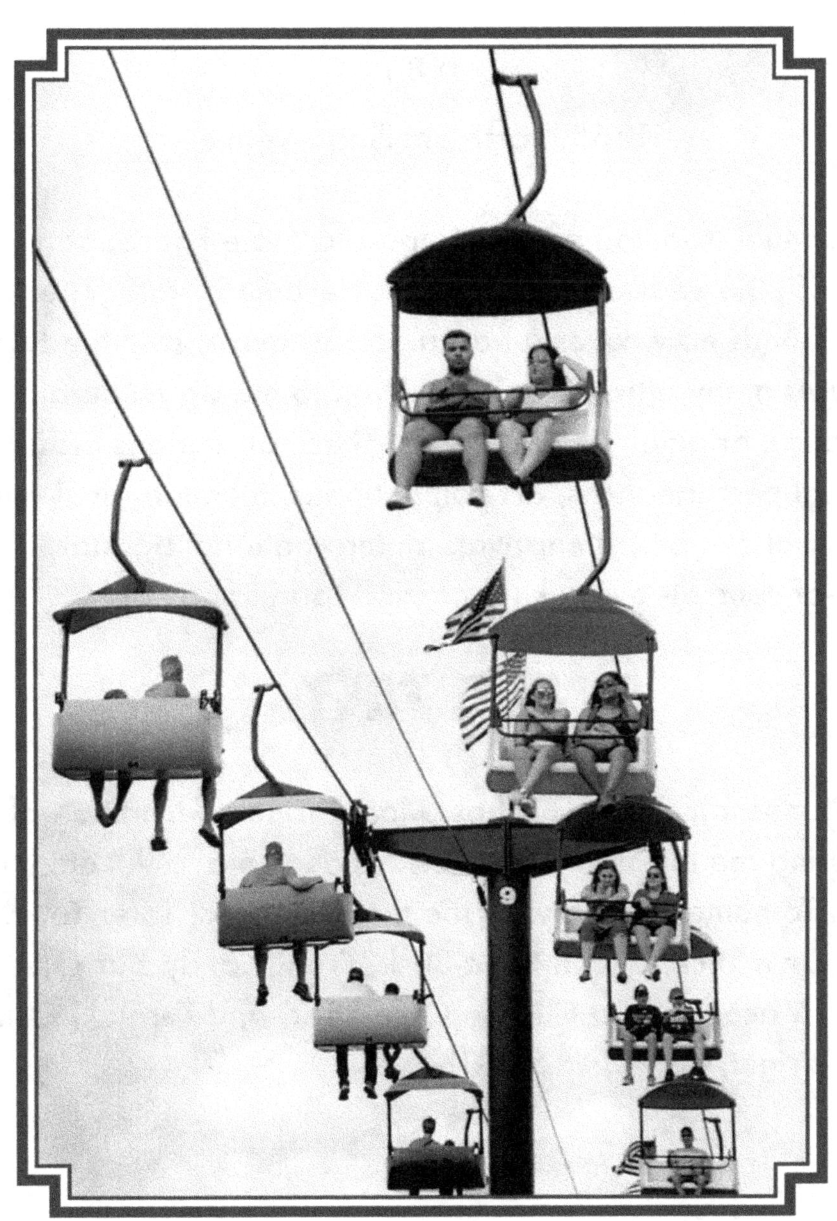

MINNESOTA STATE FAIR

- 1885 -

1265 North Snelling Avenue

The annual tradition of the Minnesota State Fair began
in 1859, the year after Minnesota became a state. The
fairgrounds now cover an area of 320 acres, and the fair
features many attractions in addition to the agricultural
exhibits it originally emphasized. These attractions include:
musical performances, art competitions, technological and
industrial exhibits, a carnival, an international bazaar,
and—of course!—every kind of fried food imaginable.

- FUN FACT -

The Minnesota State Fair has a long-standing tradition of
featuring the latest and greatest foods "on a stick" each
year. To name just a few of the many options: Tater Tot Hot
Dish On-a-Stick, Bacon On-a-Stick, Fried Candy Bar On-a-
Stick, Macaroni and Cheese On-a-Stick, and Teriyaki Ostrich
(that's right, also On-a-Stick!).

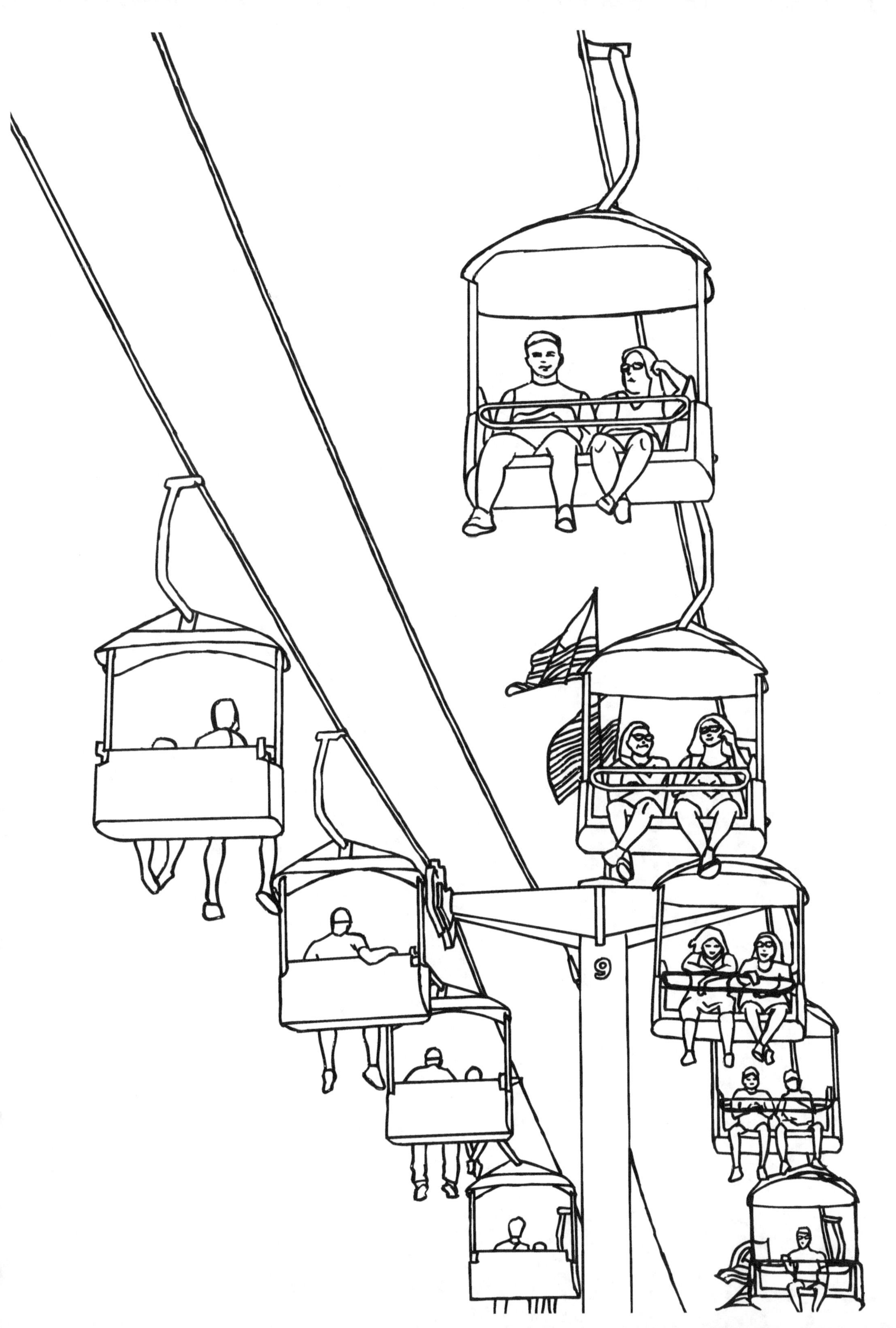

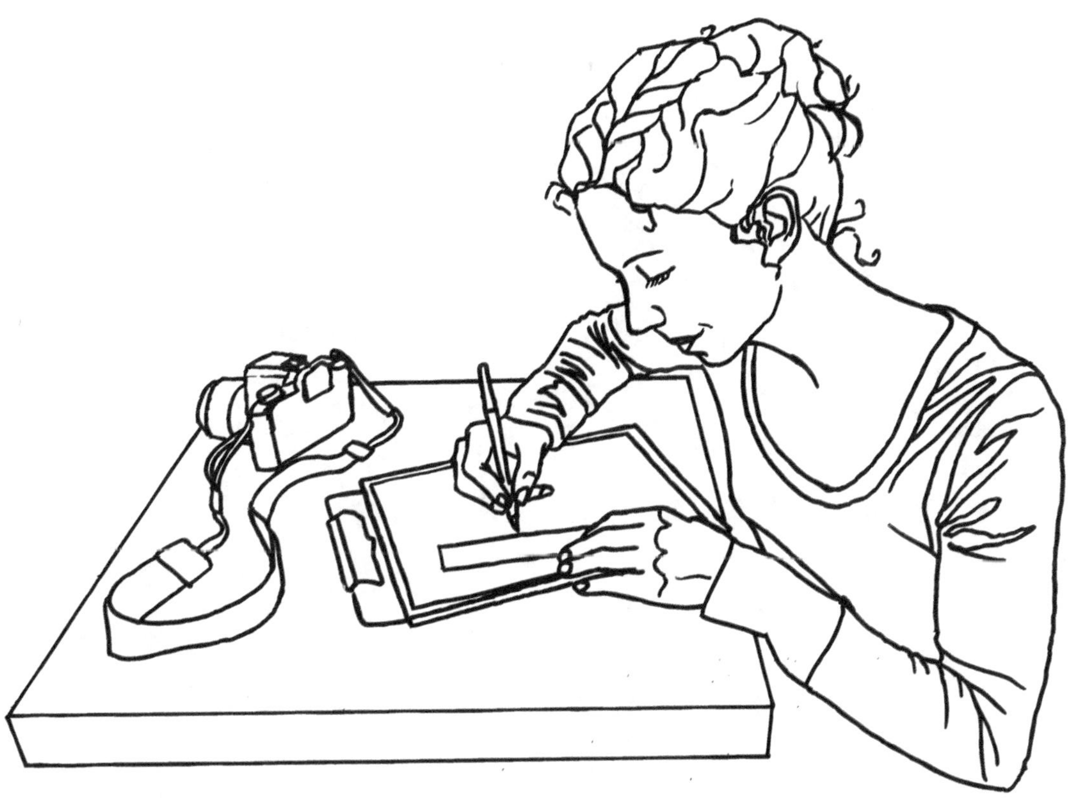

ABOUT THE AUTHOR

By the age of two, drawing instruments were already a staple
of M. Funk's existence. She would toddle around her childhood
home lugging a pen and a clipboard with her everywhere;
that's because anytime was a good time to plop down and draw
squiggly circles whose ends always met. By the age of eight,
M. possessed her very own 35mm film camera and had already
begun to document her entire life and the lives of everybody else.
By the age of eleven, M. had already started her second small
business (and certainly not her last)!

M. Funk is now an adult (sort of) and currently lives in Minneapolis
when she's not away exploring distant shores. These days she is
busy devising ways to bring together as many of the things that
she loves as possible, including: drawing, photography, business,
writing, architecture, history, travel, people, and humor.